C000246416

Rose E Faulkner

Joseph Sidney Hill

First Bishop in Western Equatorial Africa

Rose E Faulkner

Joseph Sidney Hill
First Bishop in Western Equatorial Africa

ISBN/EAN: 9783744753272

Printed in Europe, USA, Canada, Australia, Japan

Cover: Foto ©ninafisch / pixelio.de

More available books at **www.hansebooks.com**

From Photograph by Hanna, Queen Street, Auckland.]

Your loving brother in Him

J. J. Hill.

JOSEPH SIDNEY HILL

FIRST BISHOP
IN WESTERN EQUATORIAL AFRICA

BY

ROSE E. FAULKNER

Author of "A Portrait from God's Picture Gallery," "Temperance in the Light of the Cross," etc.

With an Introduction
BY THE RIGHT REV. BISHOP STUART
(Late of Waiapu)

LONDON
H. R. ALLENSON
30, PATERNOSTER ROW
1895

LOAN STACK

Printed by Hazell, Watson, & Viney, Ld., London and Aylesbury.

For all who love and honour

"Those whom the Spirit's dread vocation severs
To lead the vanguard of Christ's conquering host;
Whose toilsome years are spent in brave endeavours
To bear His saving Name from coast to coast;—

"Those whose bright faith makes feeble hearts grow stronger,
And sends fresh warriors to the great campaign,
Bids the lone convert feel estranged no longer,
And wins the sunder'd to be one again"—

THIS STORY OF ONE

WELL DESCRIBED IN THESE LINES IS WRITTEN

IN THE HOPE THAT IT MAY PROVE TO SOME

AS A TRUMPET CALL.

CONTENTS

INTRODUCTION

INTRODUCTION

HAVING been asked to write some reminiscences of Bishop Hill during the period of his missionary labours in New Zealand, I thankfully avail myself of the opportunity of bearing testimony to his singleness of aim and high standard of devotedness during all those years that I enjoyed his intimate friendship. His most marked characteristic was what has been happily said of another—"an incorrigible unselfishness." He would spare himself no trouble or pains to be of service to others, and be ever ready to take the lowest room and eager to choose the heaviest end of the stick, so that he might relieve another of its weight. "Bear ye one another's burdens, and so fulfil the law of Christ," was a rule he continuously exemplified. Many instances of this unselfishness occur to my recollection in the years he served in my own diocese of Waiapu, and subsequently during the latter portion of the time he spent in New Zealand, when engaged in Home Mission work in the diocese of Auckland. As a natural result of his ready and active sympathy, he was continually resorted to by the distressed in mind, body, and estate, who ever found that he had an ear to listen, a heart to feel, and a hand to help. He had versatility of talent in a remarkable degree, and this, combined with his wide sympathy, enabled him to take up with untiring energy and success many different branches of work. I have often heard him described in Colonial phrase as "a good all-round man." These natural endowments of character proved of eminent service in the Home Mission work, which in a large bustling city like Auckland brought him into contact with all sorts and conditions of men. It was there in the crowds that gathered in the old Opera House, now the City Hall, on a Sunday night, that I have listened to some of his most pathetic appeals, adapting the old, old story of the Cross, by various telling illustrations and anecdotes, to the mixed multitudes of careworn men and women, many of whom were strangers to the inside of any ordinary place of worship.

Sunday, with its regularly recurring four services,

was no day of physical or mental rest to him, for in the morning was his service at Mount Eden Gaol, in which, as Honorary Chaplain, he took so keen an interest; at 11 a.m. a Church Service at Remuera, a suburb some miles distant; at 3 p.m. his lecture on Christian doctrine at the Young Men's Christian Association Rooms, and the Theatre Service at night. It was at these afternoon lectures that he was to be heard at his intellectual best. The Y.M.C.A. Hall, the erection of which, with the commodious premises of which it formed part, was due to his energy and enterprise, was a spacious and admirably arranged room for public meetings. In the body of the hall and gallery were placed five hundred chairs, and on the wide platform was room for an orchestra and speakers. These Sunday afternoon lectures were specially designed for the instruction of truth-seeking inquirers, and for the answering of objections to the Christian faith. Many subjects of social and religious importance were discussed. Those who were troubled with doubts or difficulties were invited to send in previously written questions, which the lecturer would answer so far as he could. These questions were not always, as may well be imagined, the expressions of "honest doubt," but put on purpose to embarrass and harass the lecturer; but his ready and apt replies turned the tables on the questioners, and his unfailing good-humour and unruffled temper pleased and propitiated, even when he failed to convince and to silence. I have listened to many able and distinguished missionaries, who excelled in bazaar preaching, arguing with those who encountered them in the market-place, but I do not remember ever hearing anything better than J. S. Hill's dexterous and ready replies, or to have witnessed a more imperturbable temper than his. The promise so comforting to every missionary was fulfilled to him: "Thou shalt hide them in the secret of Thy presence from the pride of man; Thou shalt keep them secretly in a pavilion from the strife of tongues" (Psalm xxxi. 20). Many were the touching testimonies to the esteem in which he was held by all classes of the Auckland public, when he was about to leave them to return to England. And deep and widespread was the feeling of a sad personal loss which pervaded the community to which he and his like-minded wife had so greatly endeared themselves by their abounding in every good word and work when the sad tidings reached Auckland that Bishop and Mrs. Hill had died on their way to the Niger. I was myself in the northern capital when the cablegram was received, and can vividly recall the universal mourning it caused. "Lovely and pleasant in their lives, and in death they were not divided," were the words and the thought that seemed to express the universal feeling. Our veteran missionary—now also gone home—the Venerable Dr. Maunsell, met me at his door when he had just heard of the sad event. We exchanged our greetings of sympathetic grief, and then, with a bright look upward, the aged saint spoke a word of comfort that I felt indeed was fitly spoken then: "*God will work His own work in His own way.*"

To that we say Amen, and would only add, "The will of the Lord be done"!

EDWARD C. STUART,
Bishop.

BATOUM,
September 25th, 1894.
En Route for Persia,

CHAPTER I

BOYHOOD AND YOUTH

"*First the blade.*"—St. Mark iv. 28.

"*What sages would have died to learn*
Now taught by cottage dames."

Keble.

CHAPTER I

BOYHOOD AND YOUTH

JOSEPH SIDNEY HILL was born on December 1st, 1851, at the village of Barnack, near Stamford. Very little is known of his early years ; but the meagre outline of his childhood is consistent with, if it does not suggest, its later development. He sprang from the people—from that sturdy, independent, God-fearing peasantry which is the backbone of the English race. His father was a builder, and so too was the son in the higher branches of constructive policy and spiritual edification. Of Henry Hill nothing is known, for he died through an accident at the early age of twenty-five. But he committed the charge of his fatherless boy and girl to his own saintly mother, of whom doubtless he was the worthy child. A pleasant picture is drawn for us of those days of childhood. The grandmother, who had opened her heart and home to the young widow and her children, was a woman of sterling piety who lived upon her Bible. She took personal supervision of this part, at least, of her little grandson's studies ; and, during his sojourn under her roof, a period covering the most important years as far as impressions are concerned—from three to nine—the foundations were laid, and deeply laid, of that scriptural knowledge which in after years made him such a real teacher. But more than this. Many a divine has been early instructed in the Word of God, and has become narrow, bigoted, dogmatic. This old grandmother might have been of the severe, puritanical type, and the Bible might have been associated in her grandson's mind with long, weary tasks, with punishment lessons and gloomy Sundays. Far otherwise does the sweet, genial personality strike us as she stands out in the memory of the very few who can speak of those days of childhood. We do not gather that the little Joseph was spoilt, but there is no doubt his early years were very free and happy. A bright, winning, manly boy, with a hearty, ringing laugh, passing the greater part of his time in play in the old-fashioned garden attached to his grandmother's home, leading his little sister into all kinds of mischievous pranks no doubt, yet always generous, truthful, affectionate —such is the picture of Joseph Hill, which we, who knew and loved him later in life, *feel* to be a true portrait. No dwarfed and stunted childhood could have developed into the virile ripeness we knew. The merry laugh—we hear it still—it was always a boyish laugh—no cares could dim, no sorrows quench the fountain of pure gladness in that most wholesome nature.

The anecdotes of his boyhood are few; such as there are all bear witness to the same characteristics. When quite a little fellow he became embroiled in a fight with a boy much older and bigger; it was in the defence of his little sister, whom the bully had teased and run off with her hat. Little Joseph sprang at the aggressor without a moment's hesitation, and would have probably got the worst of it had not a gentleman who was passing separated the boys; and naturally enough, hearing the story, he applauded the little champion.

The grandmother kept bees, which the children were never tired of watching. One day they were very much interested in noticing how the worker bees, attacked, we may suppose, like other creatures, with an occasional fit of idleness, refused to leave the hive, though driven out again and again by the drones. Little Joseph's patience becoming exhausted, he got a stick, and, putting it in the hive, stirred up the lazy bees. The result can be imagined; the child was fearfully stung, and ever after was the object of their attacks. But he did not cease to visit them, and would supply them with water, putting moss and ferns in the plates lest they should drown themselves!

Only for a brief season may we think of him in that bright country home, among the old-fashioned flowers that the bees love, climbing the trees where birds had made their lofty home, earning many a tumble (once a broken collar-bone), and perhaps many a scolding--and then the scene changes.

At nine years of age it became necessary for the widow's son to be set in the way of earning his living, and a friend of the family procured his admission to the Orphan Working School at Haverstock Hill, London. The change must have been great to the country child brought up by womenkind; but he brought to the ordeal fixed principles, ambition, and industry. No record remains of his school life; we only know that he passed through it unscathed, and rose to be head of the school.

At fourteen Joseph Hill was apprenticed to a trade, and took every opportunity of pursuing his studies. At this epoch we hear of his first friendships. He became deeply attached to a young man of the name of Sidney, whose name he adopted in addition to his own from the time of his confirmation. The early death of this young friend was one of the determinating influences in his career. But it was the Rev. Alexander Burton, of Trinity Church, Southampton, to whom belongs the honour of having discerned the latent possibilities in young Hill, and of fostering his love of learning and desire to improve himself. Mr. Burton personally directed and assisted him in his studies. These combined influences stimulated the desire, doubtless implanted long before by his grandmother, who was intensely interested in missionary work, to devote his life and powers to carrying the Gospel to the heathen.

At this time the orphan lad had no home. An uncle with whom he had been in the habit of spending his school holidays was dead, and his mother was living as housekeeper in a family. One day she was startled by receiving a letter from her son, informing her of his earnest wish to be a missionary, and also telling her that if he could pass one more examination he would be able to enter the C.M.S. Preparatory Home at Reading.

It was a heavy blow. "He was the only son of his mother, and she was a widow"; yet she could not refuse her consent. She took refuge in the difficulty of the examination, and, assuring herself that he could not pass it, promised not to oppose his wishes.

He did pass, and in 1872 he entered at Reading. Two years later he began his final course of training at the Church Missionary College, Islington, under the Rev. W. H. Barlow.

During all these years there had been a steady growth in the Divine life, a constant response to the Holy Spirit's teaching, a conscious appropriation of grace.

No one preached conversion more clearly or forcibly than Bishop Hill; but he never remembered any marked crisis in his own spiritual history. He had early learnt that wisdom's ways are ways of pleasantness, and as he grew up his heart, like an opening flower, expanded Godwards, so that it may be truly said of him, that as he grew in years he grew in grace.

It was during those years at Islington that he began the evangelistic work for which he was specially fitted, and in which he was all his life used by God to a remarkable degree. In ministrations to the sick and suffering he first met her who was destined to be henceforth the partner of his life of service, for which she was already prepared by the willing choice of her youth.

Joseph Hill's ordination took place on St. Barnabas' Day, 1876, at St. Paul's Cathedral. Among the deacons ordained at the same time was Robert Warren Stewart, also subsequently distinguished in missionary work. The two young men were at Islington together, and there formed a life-long friendship.

Events now crowd thickly in our young missionary's life. On July 4th of the same year came his dismissal, with that of other missionaries, for Africa, and on July 31st his marriage with Lucilla Leachman, who faithfully shared his labours and sufferings, and died within a few hours of her beloved husband.

The course of true love had not run quite smoothly for the young couple. There had been some natural opposition on the part of the bride's family, both on account of disparity of social position and also from the dangers of the missionary calling.

To remove misunderstanding about the latter Joseph Hill wrote the following letter to the Rev. F. Leachman, her brother :—

"C.M.S. College, Islington,
"*May 8th*, 1876.

"Dear Sir,—

". . . I am fully alive to all the objections that may naturally arise from the work before us, the trials of parting, etc., the dangers and difficulties of every missionary of the Cross, but the only point necessary to my mind is, first, entire and whole-hearted devotedness to our blessed Lord, and then for one another. I think, in fact know, this exists. We are both children of God, heirs of God, and joint-heirs with Christ Jesus. Washed in the Blood of the Lamb and having already the seal of our redemption and adoption within ourselves, constrained by the love of Christ we cannot live unto ourselves, but must live unto Him that hath died for us. Being called of God to be an ambassador for Christ to the perishing souls in heathendom, I dare not, I would not if I could, do other than go forward, trusting His Almighty power to be our strength in our perfect weakness. I can offer her no social distinction, no exalted worldly position, no wealth or worldly honour, nothing but a true, warm, loving heart, and that she knows full well I wholly give her. . . .

"I conclude from your letter that whatever may have been your first impressions in regard to our engagement, whatever your objections, all is so far right that you consider it a *bonâ-fide* engagement now. I have only one word to add, and that is, I am sure you will never live to rue the day when you gave up your sister to the highest and most glorious work under heaven. If, instead of looking at the difficulties and trial of parting, you just give her entirely into the Lord's hands, and trust Him to keep her, all will be well.

"Asking a very special interest in your prayers at this important season, and trusting that, whatever may be in the future, we all, both yours and mine, may be found among that glorious and joyous throng wearing crowns decked with many a gem, to be with Him who has already washed us in His Blood, where there is neither marrying nor giving in marriage, neither sorrow nor pain, and where parting is unknown,

"Believe me,

"Yours very affectionately,

"JOSEPH HILL."

On June 20th the Rev. Henry Wright sent a warm letter, conveying the Committee's sanction of the marriage, which took place on July 31st at St. Mary's, Islington.

A month before their wedding, Mr. Hill and Miss Leachman had attended the Mildmay Conference together, and they were anxious that their honeymoon should be spent at Keswick; so the wedding took place at eight o'clock in the morning, and at eleven the bride and bridegroom were in the train, speeding northwards. Surely no bride ever entered with more chastened feelings on the halcyon days of early married life. Thus she writes to her brother :—

". . . M. and F. seem anxious about my future, but I am so sure that the whole thing is in my Heavenly Father's hands that I am at perfect rest about it all; my happiness depends on Him, not on Joseph Hill, so I have not a fear.

I can only feel it a tremendous privilege to be sent out to teach the dear little black chicks. Whenever death comes, it will be to me only (as some one so beautifully said) 'a rough messenger sent to call me home.' Human friends may fail, God never can. The only dark spot about it is leaving the dear ones in England."

Truly the Heavenly Father was early preparing His child, and her willingness to meet death for the "tremendous privilege" of work in Africa was yet to be put to a triumphant test.

CHAPTER II

FIRST VISIT TO AFRICA

"*First the blade, then the ear.*"—ST. MARK iv. 28.

"*Most happy is he who in his youth gives himself up to this guidance (of the Heavenly Friend), for he alone in this life can realise the fulness of the Divine scheme and plan. From the moment of his birth the love and will of God has surrounded such an one. He begins with* γένεσις, *the birth of all things by the breath of God; he ends with the* τέλος κυρίου, *the finished purpose of the will of the Lord.*"—J. H. SHORTHOUSE.

CHAPTER II

FIRST VISIT TO AFRICA

ON October 14th, 1876, the little party of missionaries left Liverpool in the *Bonny*, and thus the first experiences were recorded :—

"MY OWN DEAREST MOTHER,—

"We have now been six days out at sea, and passed the worst part of our journey. On Sunday we had no service; all felt the effect of the roll, and during the night the wind was anything but pleasant. All the time I could but think of that one passage, 'He holdeth the sea in the hollow of His hand,' and prayed that He who said, 'Peace, be still,' would keep us in perfect peace. In fact I made up a short sermon on those words in case I had to preach. There is one little black girl on board, with a sharp but interesting face. . . . The Lord is able to keep us both. He will not leave us comfortless, but will give us the Spirit of comfort. May God Himself take care of and bless you. With best love,

"Your ever loving children,

"JOSEPH AND LUCILLA."

This little African girl was adopted by Mrs. Hill,

and afterwards educated in England. An account of her has been published.

The next letter is from Fourah Bay, Sierra Leone:

" . . . The scenery is so lovely here; we are sitting in the verandah of the Fourah Bay Institution. The Mountains of the Moon, which stretch right across Central Africa and end at Sierra Leone, are in the background, and in the foreground are two immense cotton trees and a large number of cocoanut palms. On our right and left is Fourah Bay, for this Institution is on a point of land stretching out into the sea, and just a little way out is the *Bonny*.

" Mr. Sunter, whom you will remember, was astonished beyond expression to see Miss Leachman, as he calls me, on the West Coast. He has been so kind, and made us so welcome. After board ship one does appreciate the large airy bedrooms, good food, delicious tea, nice bath with plenty of water. Then the beautiful flowers and lovely scenery! It really is a treat after a fortnight's sea-sickness. Mr. Sunter keeps saying what a treat it is to have English people, and this when he is taking the place of six men! It is, however, vacation time with his own students. We have just had prayers; the remaining students all came in, with their gowns on: such a fine set of men. The grounds of the College extend down to the sea, and they have built a stone wall, so that the sharks can be kept out when the water comes in, and it forms a large basin for bathing. You can, however, only bathe at high water. Freetown, where we landed, is about two miles off. Mr. Sunter took us to the Mission House; the women in chairs something like bath-chairs, as it is not wise for women to walk at first. The streets of Freetown are very wide, with grass growing pretty well all over them. There is just a beaten footpath, and the ground is very uneven, with a number of half-starved looking pigs and dogs lying about. The streets swarm with people, almost entirely natives, most of them looking really picturesque in their different native dresses.

"The *Bonny* will be sailing again at nine, so I must hastily close. . . ."

We next find our missionaries at Leke, a station sixty miles east of Lagos. Their house in the mission compound was built about eleven feet above the ground, the space underneath being boarded and used as a store-room. The house consisted of five rooms, with piazzas and doors always wide open; for the life of a missionary in Africa, as in China, is a public life, and subject to invasion from all causes—from spiritual inquiry to coming to see the time of day! The roof was thatched with palm leaves, which were found to be cooler than felt or iron. In the compound were also the schoolmaster's cottage, the kitchen, and a hut for the "boys" to sleep in.

Here there seemed every prospect of a happy work, but it was not to be. On the morning of November 22nd, about six o'clock, Mrs. Hill persuaded her husband to take a dip in the sea, neither being aware of the danger from the surf. A few minutes afterwards she heard a cry, and saw from the verandah that he was out of his depth, and, with his arm thrown up, was crying aloud for help. One can picture the agony of the young wife as she rushed frantically for assistance. The veteran missionary Mr. Hinderer was with them, and, though ill and suffering, he hastened to the Commandant's house close by and got a number of Gold Coast men who happened to be there—strong men and splendid swimmers. Meanwhile the young missionary was battling alone in the surf; and, as moment after moment passed, each seeming like an hour, and strength grew weaker, he realised for the first time the imminence of death. Often has he described the awfulness of that brief waiting time, and its deeper experiences coloured his after-view of the unseen world. Often in his subsequent career he stood face to face with the last enemy, but the horror of death was past. It was twenty minutes before the brave rescuers were able to reach him and bring him safe to shore; and even then the agonised wife, praying at his bedside, could hardly believe that his life would be spared. It is said that the native who brought him in had sworn to take the life of the first white man he should meet! But it was not "in perils by water" that that young life was to be forfeited. Nevertheless the fright brought on fever with both. Old Mr. Hinderer was ill himself and unable to nurse them, and the natives were little help. Not understanding English and unable to prepare English food, they made poor nurses, and our young missionaries' first experiences of African fever were by no means pleasant. The natives meant well by them; we find them on the Sunday after the accident standing up in Church after the service and "saluting" them for coming to Africa with many a hearty good wish for spared lives and health.

Christmas came to find Mr. Hill again in bed with fever, and his wife alone with him, the native assistants having gone out for the day.

"Suddenly a number of Kru boys and canoe-men came into the compound, all half-drunk, and danced and shouted and threw each other down in the sand, and were acting like madmen. . . . Two of them walked up into our sitting-room, and demanded money or brandy. I was unwilling to disturb Sidney, but they would not go for my asking, so I had to call him. Meanwhile more had come into the compound, and, as they bear a very bad character, it was unpleasant, to use the mildest term. However, Sidney sent me into the bedroom, and then peremptorily ordered them off, telling them he would not give them a penny, however long they waited. They did wait some time; but, finding Sidney determined, they left, and went into the Commandant's house, where his black woman treated them with a warm welcome. . . ."

We next find Mr. and Mrs. Hill entertaining a little party of natives—apparently a New Year's feast. There were speeches on both sides, the young missionary, with characteristic frankness, returning the compliments of his black friends with some very plain speech about the besetting sins of Africa. Fifty had asked for baptism; but there was gross sin to be dealt with before he could entertain the application even of the most urgent.

The condition of things even in the Church itself

was far from satisfactory. Baptised Christians, even Sunday School teachers, were found to be living in open sin; and these men, being well off and in good positions, were difficult to attack. Bishop Crowther, who a few years before had given such a sanguine description in England, expressing a hope that the Native Church would soon be able to dispense with the help of missionaries from England, was beginning to find out his mistake, and was about to apply to the Church Missionary Society for English pastors for the Niger, where then there were only natives. The prospect was one of, at least, difficulty and trouble; yet the following letter—one of, alas! the very few of Mr. Hill's own that are extant—only breathes a spirit of cheerful hope:—

"LEKE, *February 14th*, 1877.

"MY OWN DARLING MOTHER,—

". . . The work here is very inviting; the people thirst for the Gospel in some parts. It is all so new to them, many never having heard of there being any future. Just imagine a man's surprise at hearing it for the first time. You have to tell him again and again, and he still doubts if you mean it. Next Sunday I intend baptising eight or ten who are real Christians—the first in this part of the country. Is it not a privilege? I am just building a schoolmaster's house. Besides seeing after the building I have to teach the native teachers, and this requires much study. I have to look after one native ordained missionary, three training for ordination, and four Scripture readers, pay them, etc. It all takes up a good deal of time. In the house we often have to do the cooking. When Loo is ill you might see me with our cook, showing him how to make a sago pudding, then buying fish of a native woman, who asks for half a crown and will take ninepence! Then there are the sick ones to attend to and some who fall away to bring back again. All this, with an ordinary clergyman's work in England for the Sunday, and classes for baptism and confirmation, forms part of our daily work for the Master.

"Your loving boy,

"JOSEPH."

It is sad to read the postscript to this letter, "Louie is still very sick." It prepares us for the next letter, announcing the move to Lagos.

" . . . I was getting very weak in Leke," Mrs. Hill writes to her sister, "and Mr. Braithwaite did not think I should recover because I could rarely keep my food down. Then Sidney got anxious about me, and when he was down at the same time, Mr. Braithwaite wrote to Mr. Maser. The kind old man came himself all the way from Lagos, bringing another canoe with him to fetch us away. We all left Leke on Thursday, and arrived in this cosy home on Saturday. I am having every kindness and attention and good nursing here. But Dr. King says that I am in a very weak state of health, and that I shall have to remain here many weeks."

Three weeks later the doctor sent in a certificate to the Finance Committee stating that both Mr. and Mrs. Hill must return to England. The former was even worse at Lagos than he had been at Leke. On March 19th a little boy was born, who only survived his birth a few hours, and Mrs. Hill was so dangerously ill that her recovery was scarcely expected. However, after a lapse of fourteen days she was able to embark on the S.S. *Africa*. Her sister had gone to Liverpool to meet the preceding boat, and her anxiety was extreme when it arrived without the expected travellers. Two days after she returned home to find a telegram explaining the delay.

The sea voyage was very beneficial to both, and they arrived in England looking and feeling quite restored to health. The Church Missionary Society, however, wished Mr. Hill to take two months' entire rest, and of that summer we have no record. Offers of curacies poured in; the two most attractive posts were the sole charge of the Rev. Melville Pym's parish during his winter mission in India, and the curacy of Holy Trinity, Richmond, under the Rev. Evan Hopkins. The latter carried the day, and in the autumn they settled down there to a time of hard but happy work, upon which Mr. Hill always looked back with the warmest interest. One of their fellow-labourers in Richmond was Miss Maud Grimston, afterwards herself a missionary and a missionary's wife. She writes thus of that time:—

"To myself, personally, he was a great blessing, and the 'inspiration' of his life follows me still; his was a life *on fire* for God and souls, and which looked far beyond the one little corner of work, to the great harvest field of the world—specially to his dear Africa. God had already called me to foreign mission work; but his words and example added fuel to the flame, and drew one so much closer to the Lord Jesus, that one could only *long* to leave all and follow Him. Bishop Hill used sometimes to join with us (the Christian working-men and me) on Sunday mornings in a small prayer meeting we had at the coffee-room, before going out to distribute tracts over the parish, and his bright cheery words pressed us on. He also began an early prayer meeting at the church, from seven to eight o'clock on Sunday mornings, for workers; and though very few attended, yet, judging by myself, it seemed to seal the day for God; the meeting with Him that early morning hour is one of the happy recollections of those Richmond Sundays. The Bishop had a very interesting Bible Reading on Prophecy at his house, as the coming of the Lord was a 'blessed hope' to both him and Mrs. Hill. I have not spoken of her, but I dearly loved her; she was always full of sympathy and sound judgment, and I valued her friendship very highly."

This was one of the friendships in which his life was rich; another was that with his vicar, the Rev. Evan Hopkins, which, unimpaired by time and distance, was happily renewed on Joseph Hill's return from New Zealand.

CHAPTER III

WORK AMONG THE MAORIS AND COLONISTS

"*Measure thy life by loss, instead of gain,*
Not by the wine drunk, but the wine poured out,
For Love's strength standeth in Love's sacrifice;
And whoso suffers most, has most to give."

H. HAMILTON KING.

CHAPTER III

WORK AMONG THE MAORIS AND COLONISTS

MISSIONARY work during this busy winter had only been in abeyance. Mr. Hill still belonged to the Church Missionary Society, and in July 1878 they decided to send him to New Zealand the same autumn. The Committee had received a special request from the Rev. T. S. Grace at Tauranga to send out a man or men to evangelise the "King" natives (especially the Waikatos), a brave and noble tribe who had been alienated from British rule by the disastrous war, and as a consequence would not sell their land or tolerate settlers among them. Mr. Grace thought if a fresh missionary came who had had nothing to do with the war, but should simply go and live at Taupo, and work from that place as a centre, the tribe might gradually be won. But in this matter both parties fell into the very uncommon error of too great promptitude. Mr. Grace finding his mistake, the Waikato district within the confiscated boundary not yet being open to Europeans, wrote to undo his request, but too late; the missionaries were already on their way. This fact will explain much that follows, and show how from the first Mr. Hill's path in New Zealand was fraught with difficulty and very special need of guidance.

On September 27th he left England, accompanied by his wife and sister-in-law, and arrived in Auckland the middle of November. After two days' rest they started again in the *Taranaki*, expecting to reach Tauranga by six o'clock the next day. It was very hot, the beginning of the New Zealand summer, and the little party stayed on deck all night, lying down but getting little sleep. A thick fog came on in the morning, and at nine o'clock they could not see twenty yards. The coast in that part is very dangerous on account of hidden rocks even in daylight, and in a fog, of course, the peril is greatly increased.

"Suddenly," writes Miss Leachman, "the Captain rushed to the wheel. . . . We saw some white foam, and with a tremendous jerk dashed on a huge rock in front of us. For a moment I felt anxious, thinking all was over, but my confidence in God never forsook me. The others, Sidney and Loo, were so calm and composed that my fears were speedily hushed. The boats were lowered as speedily as possible, but it seemed ages before they got them into the water."

Then the usual scene ensued, which makes a shipwreck on a British vessel something near akin to the sublime. Only two or three steerage passengers gave any trouble; they would, with frightful oaths, have forced themselves into the boats, but the Captain kept them back, and all the rest behaved admirably. While the water poured into the engine-room, three boats were filled with women, rowed round to the other side of the rocky island on which they had struck, and brought back for a fresh freight. We can picture the anxiety of those trembling women, waiting in the dim light on that inhospitable shore for husband and father to join them, fearing lest the ship should certainly go down before all were rescued ; scanning boat-load after boat-load, and turning away sick with suspense when the loved ones were still missing. This ordeal lasted the longest for our friends, for the two clergymen, Mr. Hill and Mr. Goodyear, were, of course, the last to leave the vessel.

All that long, dreary day they waited on the rock. It was infested with lizards, which proved very troublesome ; but, worse still, some of the men became intoxicated with the liquor they had access to. But a boat had been despatched to Tauranga, and about five o'clock in the afternoon a small steamer came to their relief and brought them to their destination.

No one who does not know New Zealand can imagine the charm of a country township such as Tauranga, with its pure light air, its lovely scenery, mountain, lake, and sea, and its abundant vegetation. Apples, plums, peaches, raspberries, damsons, lemons, etc., were all growing in the garden. It was a new life, and for a time a pleasant one. True, the young ardent missionary yearned to preach, but he was well occupied in beginning the study of Maori, giving some help in carpentering, and learning to ride, an absolutely necessary accomplishment in that part of the world. Meanwhile he waited to know his ultimate destination, as the C.M.S. had left it in the hands of the Bishop of Waiapu to arrange where he should be for the next year or two till Taupo should be open.

With the new year (1879) we find them settled in a cottage of their own in Auckland. It was a time of much proving to the young missionary. He had gone to New Zealand, sent, as he believed, by God to win the Maoris for Christ. He had found nothing but opposition and difficulty. The missionary who had been the means of bringing him out, though personally most kind and hospitable, was not slow to let him know that he was not wanted in that part of the mission field. There were only three native students to teach. In fact the reception that the rocky shore had given to their vessel was an apt illustration of what they had spiritually to experience. In a letter written long after to the Rev. C. Fenn, containing a retrospect of this period, Mr. Hill says, "I was almost broken-hearted at the reception we received." We shall remember these words when, in the last chapter of his life, we see how for the last time his tender heart was wounded in a similar manner "in the house of his friends," before he went to be comforted for ever by the once rejected Saviour.

While thus torn by doubt and disappointment, the telegram had come desiring him to return to

Auckland, and immediately he plunged into work of all kinds.

He took temporary duty at St. Matthew's Church, threw himself heartily into the work of the Young Men's Christian Association, preaching in the theatre, etc. The incumbent of St. Matthew's, who had gone home on account of health, having subsequently resigned the charge, about six hundred of the parishioners signed a petition to the Bishop and the nominators, praying for Mr. Hill's appointment.

The Bishop of Waiapu, his chief friend and adviser, did not approve of this, and Dr. Maunsell, an influential clergyman of Auckland, assured him that if he took up work in the Colonial Church he would be spoilt as a missionary to the Maoris. On the other hand, he felt he was not making progress in the language, and he knew that his work in Auckland was being owned and blessed by God. A further inducement to a settled life came on February 28th in the gift of a baby girl, christened in recognition of the parents' gratitude, Edith Theodora = beloved gift of God. But in spite of all he stuck to his commission. With the fine sense of honour that characterised him he declined the comfortable provision, the familiar routine of work, the home-life in a cultivated centre, and set himself to wait the call back into the wilderness. Rather perhaps to his surprise and a little to his mortification, the Committee at home expressed themselves as perfectly willing to set him free for this parochial work, provided that Bishop Stuart had no suitable sphere of Maori work to offer; but (to quote his own words) "I felt it impossible then to give up a work to which I had consecrated my life."

It was doubtless a relief to throw off for a time all these agitating *pros* and *cons*, and start with Bishop Stuart for a month's tour among the Maori settlements. They left Auckland on March 31st, and went first to Tauranga, and thence by steamer to Gisborne and Napier. These are flourishing Colonial towns; but at Napier they proceeded on horseback to Taupo, the headquarters of the unfriendly Kingite tribes. On the very day that Mr. Hill was preaching here to Maoris, the veteran missionary at Tauranga, Mr. Grace, was called up higher. The result of nearly seven weeks' diligent visiting convinced the Bishop that Taupo was not yet ready for a resident missionary, and they set their faces homeward.

In August 1879 Mr. and Mrs. Hill left Auckland, having been appointed by Bishop Stuart to the charge of the Wairoa in Hawke's Bay. They had greatly endeared themselves to the Auckland people, and there was great regret at their departure. A letter of warm thanks from the President and Secretaries of the Young Men's Christian Association contains the following sentences:—

"Having on your arrival amongst us identified yourself with the Association as a member, and at once entered with zeal into its work, no expenditure of time or strength has seemed to you too great in the interest of the Association, especially in connection with its evangelistic work. We join you in heartfelt thanksgiving to our loving Lord for the success which has attended those labours."

The Bishop writes as follows :—

"BISHOP'S COURT, AUCKLAND,
"*August* 18*th*, 1879.

"MY DEAR MR. HILL,—

"As you are going to leave Auckland to-day, I write to thank you for your kind and very efficient ministrations to the prisoners in the Auckland Gaol. I consider the Sunday services there among the most important in the diocese, and cannot doubt that there, if anywhere, our 'manifestations of the Spirit' will be blessed by God 'to profit withal.' Besides the prisoners in the gaol, there are many of our Auckland people who feel grateful to you, and will hear with real interest of the progress of your work in Hawke's Bay. That you may be the means whereby many souls are won to the Saviour, and are confirmed in the faith, in the wide and most interesting field of labour to which you are now called, is the earnest prayer of

"Yours faithfully,
"W. G. AUCKLAND.

"THE REV. J. S. HILL."

The little party did not go straight to their new home. They first went to Gisborne, and then to Napier, to stay with the Bishop; and during this interval Mr. Hill was examined for and admitted to priest's orders. "The Bishop," his wife notes, "seemed very pleased with his papers."

The new sphere embraced all that the ardent soul of J. S. Hill could wish in the way of opportunity for work. There were about three hundred Europeans to minister to, and a large number of Maori *pahs*, or settlements, in the neighbourhood. The resident magistrate, Mr. Baker, was a Christian man, son of a well-known clergyman in New Zealand, and he undertook to interpret to the Maoris. This kind offer was not, as it proved, altogether wise, as it prevented Mr. Hill from being forced into acquiring the language.

"The house," Mrs. Hill writes, "stands in a paddock of four acres. The rooms are small, but cosy, and there are seven of them. . . . M. (Miss Leachman) employs her time in teaching the Maori boys and girls, but finds them an erratic lot. Miss Williams had given her good help with the Maori tongue while at Napier. . . ."

The Maoris are a fine, intelligent race, but their contact with civilisation has greatly tended to their degeneration. Justice required that we should provide for their wants when we were fast crowding them out of their lands, but it is obvious enough that half-savage people, when they can get all they want without trouble, will lapse into old vices and easily acquire new ones. Peace and plenty are not unmixed blessings.

They are exempt from many local rates, and when the death of a chief, or other public event, causes a large number to travel together, the Government allows them to have free passes, or sends a special steamer to carry them to their destination. Mrs. Hill records an instance of the way in which they regard every kindness as a right. One day, while she was busy in her kitchen, a Maori came to ask for medicine. She did not answer him immediately, whereupon he went round the house, walked in at the back door, straight into the kitchen, and in a surly tone demanded food as well as medicine. The servant brought him a good meal, consisting of a large plate of meat, a third of a loaf of bread, and a large cup of cocoa. He glared at her, and said angrily, "He mea paku" (too little). However Mrs. Hill did not lose her presence of mind, but nodding to him said, "All right, my friend, that's all you'll get!" So he ate it all up, and then demanded writing-paper, envelopes, and vinegar, with which mixed goods he at length consented to depart.

Time is nothing to a Maori. When Mr. Hill invited some of the chiefs to meet the Bishop on a certain occasion, at *dinner*, six of them arrived at 7.30 a.m., and waited patiently. At the appointed hour there were twenty-one instead of the original nine—rather a strain on the resources of the Mission House, but they got enough to eat, leaving nothing, however, for the family themselves.

The following letter will give some idea of the kind of life that colonial bishops and clergy often have to live:—

"THE PARSONAGE, WAIROA,
"*March 22nd*, 1880.

"When I last wrote to you Sidney was away at Gisborne. The Bishop being anxious to get back, they started early on the Tuesday morning in a gentle rain, hoping it would turn out fine. Instead of that it kept on, and got worse and worse, and when they reached Reniga, the (Hauhau) Maori settlement, half-way from Gisborne, they were both drenched to the skin. This was at six o'clock in the evening. To their dismay the Maoris told them they could not give them a single blanket, nor any fire, and scarcely any food. It would have been madness to stay under the circumstances, and so they came on, and arrived here at 2.30 in the middle of the night, having been eighteen hours in the saddle in a heavy rain."

Mr. Hill has often spoken with great interest of the work that he was occasionally able to do in settling Maori disputes.

They showed great reverence for the Bible, from which he always read to them. On one occasion a dispute had arisen about some land, a landmark having been tampered with. He was sent for to arbitrate, and taking his Bible he read them the curses in Deut. xxvii., purposely omitting the seventeenth verse. They were much impressed, murmuring, "Amen," and "Very good." Then he summed up by solemnly reading, "Cursed is he that removeth his neighbour's landmark." The guilty persons were convicted, and the land restored.

Another time he settled a dispute by reading the story of Solomon's judgment on the living child, to which the circumstances bore some resemblance.

In the letter last quoted Mrs. Hill says :—

"To-day Sidney has gone on a difficult little journey

to Nuhaka, about twenty miles or more from here. Two tribes of natives have been quarrelling there for some time past over some land, and they intended either to-day or to-morrow to settle it by fighting. A few of the Maoris sent a message to S. to ask him if he would go and try to prevent fighting. So he and Mr. Baker started early this morning, and will not return until to-morrow night, if then. I felt anxious about him, as he will have to sleep in a wretched Maori whare, but he said to me in his cheerful way, 'The path of duty is the path of safety,' and certain it is that he is safe in God's mighty keeping and love. . . ."

The work among the Europeans was full of difficulty and discouragement. When one reads that the congregation was mostly composed of drunkards and infidels, and that there was not a man to stand by him, one can fancy that the contrast to the help and sympathy experienced at Auckland must have been very great. There were seven vestrymen and two churchwardens, but none of them were Communicants. If money was wanted for the church, the old plan had been to raise it by means of a concert, with a dance at the close. No wonder they found the people at the Parsonage too particular!

Mr. Hill tried to teach them in every possible way. He had studied medicine at College, and had a great aptitude for it. He now purchased some first-rate medical and surgical books and a thoroughly good medicine chest, and set to work in right good earnest. At all hours of the night or day he was at the disposal of the settlers, who sent for him without scruple.

He was always most uncompromising in rebuking sin, and this attendance at sick and dying beds gave him spiritual access which he never could have acquired in any other way, and his Gospel preaching on these occasions was probably more blessed with results than his plain preaching in church to people who in health and strength did not fear his warnings.

He continued his work among the sick until a new resident doctor came, and then, with his characteristic generosity, he made him a present of his chest of valuable drugs, because he said it would be unfair to give them away when the doctor had to make his living.

How he wrestled for souls in long hours when he sat beside his patient; how he suffered when a child died notwithstanding all his care, or, worse still, when an apparent penitent relapsed into sin on recovery, is only known to Him who went out to seek and to save the lost. There were bright gleams in this work: as when on one occasion he was sent for in the middle of the night to see a baby with croup, five or six miles off—a "nasty" ride in the dark; for he had the joy of comforting a mother in a dreadful state of anxiety, and pulling the baby through.

The schools took up a great deal of his time and thoughts, and on one occasion, when the

Government schoolmistress fell ill, Miss Leachman and he took the whole work upon themselves, rather than allow the school to be closed.

Another method that he adopted to interest the young people was by giving lectures on popular scientific subjects. It is most characteristic of him that, when an Easter offering of over twenty-two pounds had been raised for him, he spent nearly the whole of it in apparatus for his lectures on electricity.

With all this he did not neglect the physical side of Christian life. He started a cricket and football club, and was captain of both, as he had been at College. He was a reckless rider, and his boyish love of fun, which the hardest experiences of life never could dim, led him sometimes astray, as when he once allowed himself to be allured into a race which led to his breaking his collar-bone. He was riding with his sister-in-law. A friend had taken the children and Mrs. Hill into the country to have a day's outing and get fruit for jam. He had been delayed by school work, and, mounted on a new horse, he was making up for lost time, when he was overtaken by two of the town boys, who depreciated his new purchase, and challenged him to prove which of their steeds was superior. Our friend, put on his mettle, set off at a breakneck pace. Presently Miss Leachman, riding behind, came up to his horse without rider or saddle. It had been carelessly saddled by their boy, and the one girth had given way. Happily the accident was not very serious.

All these many-sided interests and occupations were not allowed to interfere with the constant spiritual work, both at the Wairoa and other places, with which these years were filled, and of which we will speak more at length in another chapter.

CHAPTER IV

WORK IN THE WAIROA

"*Not stirring words, nor gallant deeds alone,*
Plain, patient work fulfilled that length of life;
Duty, not glory—service, not a throne—
Inspired his efforts, set for him the strife."

CLOUGH.

CHAPTER IV

WORK IN THE WAIROA

MISSIONS—we need not explain the special application of that very useful word—were not so common fifteen years ago as they are now. In a new country, where life is for the most part hard, any change is welcome, and there is never any difficulty in getting an audience. Although Mr. Hill always threw himself with ardour into anything that he undertook—for it was not in his nature to do things by halves—it was especially in a mission that he found the freest scope for his powers and energy. His versatile gifts enabled him to carry out everything that came to him to do, and to carry it out well; but he was *par excellence* an evangelist. His success lay in his own firm belief in the Gospel he preached to change lives as well as hearts. His style and manner improved markedly as time went on; but from the first his plain, straightforward preaching was blessed with definite results wherever he went. Up to the time that he left England in November 1893—never, alas! to return—a mission never failed to cheer him, even when most careworn and depressed.

In May 1880 he accompanied the Bishop of Waiapu on a mission to the town of Waipukurau, leaving Mr. Goodyear, who was afterwards associated with him in the work, in charge of the Wairoa. It was a most successful time. He had Bible readings every morning, evangelistic services every evening, and some also at the hospital. Numbers of letters poured in testifying to definite blessing received. One gentleman said Waipukurau was quite a changed place since the mission. The young missioner was always very strong upon restitution and practical proofs of blessing received, and he had on this occasion a very cheering instance of the fruits of his teaching. A young man who came to the services was led to see that the occupation in which he was engaged was not one that he could continue to the glory of God, and he decided to give it up, although it was for him the loss of a good situation of £200 a year. After the mission we find that the charge of Waipukurau was suggested to Mr. Hill, but declined. The following letter from a lady in the vicinity will show that there was good *after*-work to the mission. After speaking of some cards of memorial, she says :—

"I trust the best remembrance will be the love of Christ shed abroad in their hearts, constraining them to live not to themselves, but to Him who 'loved them and gave Himself for them.' While writing this, it has struck me,

Why should I speak only in the third person? It is not only the new recruits enlisted under the banner of the Cross who have to thank our Father for last week's privileges. What 'times of refreshing' these services have been to the older soldiers! It is so cheering to go from house to house and hear how the 'old, old story' has come home with new power to the hearts of the Lord's own people. At one time we had far too much distrust and suspicion between Churchmen and Presbyterians; now it has all disappeared. There seems a great wish for the establishment of a weekly prayer meeting (at the Parsonage if Mr. S—— cannot come out at night), where all shall meet on the common ground of love to our Redeemer. I hope it will be carried out.

"Miss D—— and Miss G—— will accompany Mr. S—— on Thursday to the hospital; and there is a project talked of too for Sunday, that after school three or four of the young people shall go and sing at the hospital. This plan originated with the G.s; they tried it before the mission services, and hope to make it a regular engagement now. You will, I know, pray that we may all 'grow in grace'; and you may be sure you will be long remembered in prayer. . . ."

That autumn a pleasant little event occurred to bring further cheer to the little party at Wairoa Parsonage. Mr. Tonge from Birmingham, so well known now in connection with the C.E.Z.S., came to New Zealand on a voyage for his health. Meeting Mr. Baker at Wellington, he was persuaded to go on to the Wairoa to see the work among the Maoris. So, accompanied by his wife and sister-in-law, he arrived at the Hills' house, to their great delight. Three horses having been borrowed for their use, many pleasant spring days (it was then September) were spent in visits to the Maori settlements, either by horse or boat.

The next event in our friend's life was the birth of another little girl in November.

In the beginning of December Mr. Hill went to Auckland to hold a special mission, and, as usual, his work there was so blessed that it drew forth the following letter. We insert it here; for, though he could not at that time accept the offer, it opened the way for the arrangement which afterwards secured his services for Auckland.

"AUCKLAND, *December 22nd*, 1880.

"MY DEAR BROTHER,—

"Since you left Auckland a few friends, who think there is a good field in Auckland for the exercise of your special qualifications in the Master's service, have conferred together, and, after careful consideration and prayer, concluded to address you a letter expressive of their views, and I was requested to be the writer."

After a few remarks the letter proceeds with the following offer:—

"That you be engaged for twelve months for evangelistic work in Auckland and its neighbourhood, such as the holding of special services, church missions, and city mission work, at a guaranteed salary, the matter to be managed by a representative committee. After receiving your reply, if at all favourable, we propose to bring the matter before the Y.M.C.A. committee (as all denominations are there represented) for advice as to the formation of the working committee, but not that the work shall be directly under the control of the Y.M.C.A., or be any charge upon its funds; but its organisation would in many ways be useful in connection with such a work as is now contemplated. We have no desire to suggest anything that would place you in an awkward position with reference to the Church to which you belong, but we imagine that what we propose will be perfectly consistent with the position you hold as a minister of that Church. If not, of course you will not hesitate at once to say so. Our sole object and desire is that souls may be saved and our Redeemer glorified; and, if what has been put into our hearts is of the Lord, we doubt not it will be so made clear to you, and if not we trust it will be made equally plain. With our united prayers that you may be guided by the Divine Spirit to a right decision,

"Believe me, my dear Mr. Hill,

"Yours in Christ,

"THOMAS B——.

"In your reply please be as full and free as possible, keeping back nothing you have on your mind to write."

This letter shows how thoroughly the young missionary's evangelistic work had been appreciated by earnest people in Auckland. Indeed nothing is more remarkable in the Colonies than the earnest effort that godly men are ever making for the good of their countrymen. Sin abounded in Auckland, as in other new cities to which drift evil-doers from all countries. The class that "makes haste to be rich" were of course, as ever, indifferent to religion. But the energy and "go" to be found in perfection in colonists were conspicuous also in Christian workers. When one considers that all Churches are voluntary, and, as far as means go, on the same footing, it is astonishing to note the rapidity of church-building, the number of denominations ably represented, the organisations at work and liberally supported in a town like Auckland, which has passed through such terrible financial depression.

Mrs. Hill writes, March 18th, 1881 :—

"Sidney is off on horseback to see some patients. He has had many bad cases lately. In reference to one of these the doctor at the Napier Hospital wrote to him: 'I conclude you must at some time have studied medicine; at all events the patient has to thank you for a very correct appreciation and treatment of his disease.' I am afraid you will feel sorry when I tell you that he has finally declined the living of Waipukurau. It was rather difficult for him to refuse, as the dear Bishop put it as a personal favour to himself. The truth is Sidney is cut out for an evangelist. A dear saintly lady told Sidney he ought not to go to Waipukurau, and he ought not to stay here much longer; she said he ought to be working as an evangelist, or be in a city where he would have hundreds to preach to, instead of twenty or thirty people. The Bishop has asked him to go and hold an eight days' mission at Taradale in three weeks' time, so he will be away again soon. As soon as the people heard of his leaving they said they would not let him go. One of the settlers, Mr. P——, called on me about it. He said that *Sidney's living here had raised the value of land all over the district.* I told him that money had nothing whatever to do with it."

"*April* 15*th*, 1881.

"Sidney has lost one patient of acute bronchitis, a dear little boy seven years old. He was with little Edwin for hours each day he was ill, and when he died he died in Sidney's arms, *alone*, for his mother was so terrified she left the room. She told Sidney she was perfectly satisfied that everything was done that could be done, but Sidney felt his death dreadfully and could hardly get through the funeral service. All the Sunday School children went (it was Sunday afternoon), and all Wairoa was there. He spoke a few words on the text, 'Is it well with the child? and she answered, It is well.'

"Sidney is now at Taradale holding a mission, which we hear is a very successful one. This sort of work always cheers him up so tremendously, and I cannot wonder, for he is so much blessed. A short time ago he received a most touching note from a clergyman who had been blessed in his services held in Auckland just before Christmas. The clergyman had got to be quite without hope either as regards this world or the next. He went *by chance* to one of the mission services, and he said Sidney's address sent through his whole being such a thrill of hope as he had not experienced for years. . . . He was so completely overcome that evening that he said he could not possibly speak to Sidney, much as he longed to do so and to get a grasp of his hand."

We read that winter of endless journeyings all over the country, preaching, lecturing, visiting the sick, etc. Sometimes there was a droll recognition of his varied powers and opportunities, as in the following item of news: "The Government have sent to Sidney asking him to vaccinate the Maoris at 2*s*. 6*d*. a head!"

The beginning of a new year was marked with another accident, not to himself, but to the Bishop. Mrs. Hill thus relates it :—

"On February 25th the Bishop arrived here overland with his daughter. His horse had died, and he had to look out for another. Eventually he offered to buy Sidney's—the new bay. Sidney insisted on getting on the animal to try him before the Bishop did so. The horse bucked with him, but he kept his seat, and then gently got off and brought Bob back, saying he would not allow the Bishop or any of us to get on him, as he saw he was unsafe. The Bishop, however, did, and the instant he got outside the gate, Bob bucked, and bucked, and bucked again, and then managed to dash him off against the fence. For a moment we thought he must have been killed, but he got up and came into the house. The doctor was sent for, and said the Bishop's collar-bone was broken."

This was on March 4th. The next day Mr. Goodyear was ordained priest, for although the Bishop was all strapped up and suffering much pain, he insisted on holding the service.

For some time Mr. Hill had been contemplating a change of work, and now that his coadjutor was in priest's orders, there was no reason why he should not be left in charge of the Wairoa.

The Vicar of Gisborne had left his living for three months (ending in his resignation), and the Bishop wished Mr. Hill to go and officiate there. Gisborne was called Poverty Bay by Captain Cook, because when he landed there he could get nothing from the natives—no food, nor even roots—and was obliged in consequence to sail away. It is an inappropriate name for such a fertile district. The town consists chiefly of one long and very wide street, well planted with trees. The buildings were sparsely scattered along it then; no doubt it has filled up in the course of twelve years, but even in 1882 there were 3,000 inhabitants. The parish was in an unhappy and divided state, and the new pastor did not find it a bed of roses. But it was his nature to triumph over difficulties, and his kindly, loving disposition could not fail to bring peace, even when he felt it his duty to preach judgment.

There were great lamentations in the Wairoa, yet his last sermon was not a message of comfort to the faithful in his congregation, but addressed to sceptics, for a large number calling themselves so attended church to pass the time. The church was full, and the sermon made a deep impression. The next day it was talked of all over the town. One man remarked to Mrs. Hill, "We never miss the water till the well runs dry." There was only one class of persons who did not regret Mr. Hill, and that was the publicans.

The people in Wairoa and the neighbourhood sent him a testimonial. It is amusing, but not surprising, to hear that it was followed after some time by a telegram to know if it had been received. It was so like him to be deeply touched and gratified at the kindness, but quite to forget to acknowledge it.

Mrs. Hill writes from Gisborne :—

"We have a tiny little house here, but so bright and clean ; too small, however, to have a servant living in the house. Mr. A. B—— has lent Sidney such a nice horse. It seems riding is inevitable here, as the settlers live such a long distance from each other. He holds a service three Sunday afternoons at Makaraka, a town about six miles off, and the fourth Sunday at Osborne, twelve miles off. . . . Sidney is now in the full swing of heavy work. For the last fortnight he has preached or given addresses every night, and three full services generally on Sunday, the afternoon service involving a long ride."

Once more an effort was made to secure Mr. Hill's permanent services, but he had now fully made up his mind that God was calling him to evangelistic work, and he felt he should be more useful in a large centre than in a small parish where he would have the addition of pastoral work. He had not come to this decision without pain. It was natural that the Bishop should like to have him in parochial work in his own diocese. Wherever he went for missions he was loved by all classes except the idle and the vicious. Men such as are found in colonial life, hard-headed, plain-speaking folk, appreciated his thorough manliness, his entire absence of "the fear of man that bringeth a snare." They liked a man who dared rebuke their sins, and yet who was always willing to help them and identify himself with their interests. He was never quite happy in the work among the Maoris. He had not had a fair chance to master the language, and the want of it fettered him. In one letter he who never complained of any suffering of his own hints that the constant riding and exposure were developing a weakness contracted in West Africa—a sufficient reason in itself for a change of occupation. Yet he would never have given up the Maori work if his Committee at home had not encouraged him to do so. But all difficulties being at last removed, he left Gisborne at the close of the year 1882, and entered upon the work at Auckland which has made his name a household word in that populous and important city. Among the many welcomes he received none was of more importance to him as a clergyman than the following genial note from the Bishop of Auckland :—

"*October* 31*st*, 1882.

"DEAR MR. HILL,—

"I have received your letter of the 28th, and am very glad to hear that you are coming to Auckland, to care especially for those not attending any regular services. You will have my most cordial sympathy and support in this work, than which there is none more important or more honourable. Kindly let me know how soon we may expect you.

"Yours faithfully,

"W. G. AUCKLAND."

CHAPTER V

WORK IN AUCKLAND

"*First the blade, then the ear, after that the full corn in the ear.*"—St. Mark iv. 28.

"*Goodness is always soundness, and we must not endure to be contented with any standard of goodness which does not give proof of its health; and this it does only when it is cheerful, vigorous, elastic, free, hearty, hopeful, springing, gracious, delightful, beautiful, and strong.*"—Canon Scott-Holland.

CHAPTER V

WORK IN AUCKLAND

AT the close of the last decade, after the great depression in Auckland, there were so many houses to let that some streets had quite a deserted look; but it was not so in 1883, and it was some time before the continued efforts of friends could find a suitable house for the little household from Gisborne. At length, however, one was found which gave great satisfaction. It was situated on high ground, and could be reached in about ten minutes from the city.

Mr. Hill began work by taking the charge of a large church while the incumbent was absent at the General Synod. He then went to take a mission at Cambridge, which was marked by decided blessing, and sent him back to Auckland much cheered. A few months afterwards we find him in the same neighbourhood in similar work. When in Auckland the routine of daily work included the following engagements:—

Monday morning: Ministers' prayer meeting.

Tuesday : meeting for young men, sometimes social, sometimes a Bible reading.

Wednesday : a noonday prayer meeting for business men, and every alternate Wednesday evening a Bible class at Remuera (a suburb).

Thursday : an evangelistic service at the Y.M.C.A.

Friday : a large Bible class for ladies, and in the evening another at Parnell.

Sunday : a Bible class for young men, in addition to (generally) three services in Church.

Besides all this he was continually being called upon to give lectures and addresses, and to help in every good work. The homely remark, "There's not a lazy bone in Mr. Hill's body," was indeed literally true. It was his joy to serve. With all his outside engagements he gave much time to study, and one marvels at the amount of information, social, political, and scientific, which he literally poured out in his lectures. In the Colonies, if a man is to have influence, he must be in the stream of all that is going on ; a mere scholar, still less a recluse, would have no chance. There was much in the vigorous life of the young country which commended itself to the ardent spirit of Joseph Hill. He liked the simplicity and freedom of manners, the absence of humbug and cant, the readiness to give and take ; and he made friends on all sides and among all sorts and conditions of men. His quick perceptions showed him the great need there was of some one to guide the opinions of the young men on political and social questions. His own mind was by no means made up on these subjects, but he, though often carried a little far by enthusiasm, never wandered out of the way in judgment, because he always applied the rule and plummet of the Word of God to every line of thought. At one time he lectured a great deal on temperance, and went very carefully into the scientific side of the question, giving the analyses of different drinks and overwhelming his audiences with the fierceness of his indictments against alcohol. Time and experience considerably modified his views on this subject, and he held in his later years the usefulness of alcoholic drinks under certain conditions, though doubtless he never abandoned as a principle the advisability of total abstinence from the Christian point of view "for the present distress."

Drink has been so terrible an enemy to Colonial progress that it is hardly to be wondered at that any earnest man should be carried to extremes in fighting so deadly and persistent a foe.

The land question was another subject that interested him. He studied Henry George, and had the boldness to point out in public what he believed to be some of his fallacies. He had to a remarkable degree the courage of his opinions. In a society where nothing can be done in a corner, where every word uttered in public is reported in the daily papers and commented on with the utmost freedom, where paper warfare is continually waged and an untimely word will make a man unpopular, it requires no little courage to maintain what a man believes to be true even when it is diametrically opposed to the public opinion of the moment. Yet that courage was possessed by Mr. Hill, and it speaks well for the common sense of Auckland that, even when his statements took their breath away by their very audacity, their respect and admiration never failed. He allowed free discussion after his lectures; and his rare tact and kindliness managed the roughest opponents. Christian evidences were among his subjects, and many sceptics with whom he patiently argued will be found among the jewels on his crown.

In these efforts for the public good, as well as in his directly spiritual work, the busy months flew by. Early in 1884 we find him returning for a month to his old parish of Gisborne at the request of the Bishop.

"As soon as it was known in Gisborne," writes Mrs. Hill, "that Sidney was going there, with the usual Colonial hospitality he had four telegrams from different friends asking him to stay at their houses. But he and Mr. B—— had been longing to see each other all the year, so Whakawhitua was his choice. We were all asked to go, but we had already accepted an invitation to go and stay at Bishopscourt with Edith. . . .

"It was so nice having the Stuarts here; on Christmas Day the Bishop took a service on board a man-of-war."

"*April 20th*, 1884.

"Next Monday Sidney is going to Tauranga to hold an eight days' mission there. The Bishop has been preparing for it for some time past. Afterwards he is to ride with him through the Taupo district, then to Napier to hold a mission there the last week of June or first in July at the Spit, that being the busy part of Napier."

"*May 5th*, 1884.

"The mission at Tauranga was a decided success. Just as Sidney was going to the steamer a man in uniform rode up and said he wished to tell him that the services had been blessed to one of his own family. The man could hardly speak for crying. And the Bishop writes word that there have been others gathered in as the fruit of the mission.

"I went with Mr. and Mrs. A. B—— to the Hot Lakes and Pink and White Terraces—the most wonderful sight I ever beheld. I was so dreadfully sorry that Sidney could not go with us; in fact he *could* have gone, but he never will go out pleasuring unless there is absolutely no work to be done."

We refer our readers for an admirable description of these wonders of nature, so soon to be overwhelmed by earthquake, to Mr. Froude's "Oceana."

"AUCKLAND, *June 23rd*, 1884.

"MY OWN DARLING MOTHER,—

"It is a very long time since you had a line from me, and though L—— writes every mail, you say that does not do for me. Well, dear mother, I hope you will not think I have one spark the less love because I do not write; L—— seems to keep you so well posted up in everything. Since last mail I have been to a place some thirty miles from here called Bombay. We had four days' services in the church, and I gave a Bible reading every day. The church was full every night, and not sitting room the last night. Bombay is very English, the people very like those in a country village in England. No public-house here! . . .

"It is a long time since I was in R—— ; but I can, and do often, see the place in my mind's eye, and go back to the time when I was quite a boy. I have had some few changes since then, seen something of this world, and learnt an immense deal concerning that to come. A good many ups and downs since I first asked you, dear mother, if I might go out as a missionary. Grandmother gone to be with Jesus. . . .

"If you knew all the blessings one has enjoyed in one's own soul and shared with others since that day, I am sure you would not say nay if it all had to come again with all its trials. How blessed it is to look back and thus feel all has been well! His smile is worth it all. What rest, peace, and joy there is in His love! Just to lean upon Him, moment by moment, and to know all things work together for good! With very much love from all of us, and most from me,

"Believe me, my own dear mother,

"Your loving son,

"JOSEPH."

On June 24th Mrs. Hill writes:—

"We have had our house full of visitors. Mr. and Mrs. Brown, with their sister and little girl, were with us for three weeks; and while they were here Bishop and Miss Stuart came for three days, on their way to the Bay of Islands. The Bishop helped at all the services. He preached in the theatre the Sunday before last; it was densely packed, and he gave them a full clear Gospel, and said what a treat it was to preach to such eager listeners."

This winter Mr. Hill gave a great many lectures, gathering large audiences of young men. His subjects were varied. Some on natural history, illustrated by limelight, proved very attractive.

A little later we read :—

"Sidney has donned the blue ribbon; he did it because he has a very wide and strong influence amongst men in Auckland, and many of them said they would not join the Blue Ribbon Army because they did not wish to be better than Mr. Hill!"

Here is a touch which brings out the warm, affectionate character of the man :—

"M—— and T—— and the children have been staying at the Ocean Beach, Whangerui Heads, for three weeks, and a most delightful place it is. We returned rather sooner than we meant to do, because Sidney wrote such a fearfully doleful, dismal letter about the wretchedness of being alone. He waited on the wharf all night for us. The steamer was due at 12, and did not arrive till 4 a.m."

The principal event of 1885 was a visit to Australia for the purpose of holding a mission in St. Philip's Church, Sydney. It was a time of refreshing in every sense, both to mind and body. Tokens that the Holy Spirit had accompanied the word preached were not wanting in changed hearts and lives. The

Bishop of Sydney, in asking him to give one of the addresses at the Thanksgiving Service at the cathedral, said he "thanked God for the blessing that had attended the mission at St. Philip's."

The beginning of 1886 was marked by a great event in the little world of Auckland. The General Synod, which is held every three years in a different diocese, met this year at Auckland, an event which only occurs once in eighteen years. The opportunity was taken for laying the foundation stone of the new buildings of the Young Men's Christian Association. Bishop Barry, of Sydney, performed the ceremony, and made a splendid speech. There were seven bishops present, so in this case at least the Y.M.C.A. had good episcopal sanction! The twin agency, the Y.W.C.A., flourished also in Auckland (and we are glad to know still flourishes). Mrs. Hill, aided by her sister as President, did firstrate work for years among the young women.

But our ardent worker began to show signs that he was trading too much on his fine constitution and strong brain. Sitting up till two or three o'clock in the morning at hard study, and sometimes a whole night (to prepare for his lectures on infidelity), is not the way to preserve health, and in April 1886 he became ill with intense neuralgia and indigestion, which his doctor attributed to overwork. Yet he would not give in, and went to his class when quite unfit. One Sunday he preached five times, not an uncommon thing. "His class was crammed in the afternoon, and a lady who was there (ladies were admitted to the gallery only) said that the moment he had finished the infidels set on him like a pack of fiends. She was so frightened that she was obliged to come out."

Yet when he was ill Mrs. Hill writes :—

> "The infidel friends were very kind to him that day they are getting, many of them, very fond of him. They often say such blasphemous, horrible things, but he never loses his temper, and they respect him for it."

A friend who resided in Auckland at this time thus describes that particular branch of work :—

> "Among the many services which Bishop Hill rendered to Auckland, perhaps in some respects the greatest was the manly way in which he foiled and successfully fought the forces of Free-thought and Atheism which were in great activity about the time he came into our midst. A succession of peripatetic lecturers had fanned the rationalistic spirit, and had heartened the opponents of Christianity so much that a large and vigorous society was enrolled, largely attended Sunday lectures were given, and a weekly paper was established to propagate their views. Many an able sermon was preached in the churches to counteract such teaching, but the challenge to come to public discussion on the platform was unanswered. The result was that the faith of many, especially among the young men of the city, was greatly imperilied. Mr. Hill, seeing the urgency of the case, did not hesitate to go into the thick of the fight, and publicly discuss the questions in debate. No one who attended the long series of Sunday afternoon lectures which he delivered

6

in the Y.M.C.A. hall in defence of the Christian faith can ever forget the effect which they produced upon the hundreds of young men who attended. Each lecture showed a complete mastery of the subject and a skilful marshalling of arguments, and in the discussion with his opponents which invariably followed each lecture his alertness of mind and ready repartee stood him in good stead.

"But there was something more than intellectual gifts, splendid though they were, which contributed to his success. There was the intense earnestness of the man, and the transparent sincerity of his own faith in the truth for which he battled, and above all there was his loving, sympathetic nature, which never showed to better advantage than in his attitude towards the honest doubter. His influence soon began to tell, and more than one who had been prominently connected with the Rationalistic Association, and who had at first come to these meetings 'to scoff, remained to pray'; and the people generally, and especially the young men, were established in their faith. Within a very short time the Rationalistic Society dwindled rapidly, their weekly meetings were discontinued, and their journal became defunct.

"Such is an outline—a very imperfect one, I am conscious—of an imperishable service which the dearly beloved and greatly lamented Bishop rendered to the people of Auckland, and for which, as for so much else, they will ever gratefully cherish his memory."

In June of this year occurred the great catastrophe in the Lake district, with great loss of life and property. Mr. Hill was alarmed for the safety of his friend Mr. Goodyear, who had the charge of the Rotorua district, but a telegram assured him of his safety.

A thorough change being necessary for all the family, Mrs. Hill took her children to a quiet farmhouse in the country, and her husband started for a tour of united work and pleasure in Australia. He was absent seven weeks. One of his kind friends in Auckland presented him with a first-class ticket for the journey, and another with a sum of money for expenses, so he went off like a schoolboy for his holidays.

He thus records his experiences :—

"AUCKLAND, *September* 13*th*, 1886.

"My darling Edith has been talking to me about not writing to you, dearest mother; so just a word. I have been from home seven weeks in Sydney, Melbourne, and Ballarat, and had wonderful blessing in every place. God has been so very good to us all. With warmest love,

"Your loving boy,

"SIDNEY."

In September Mrs. Hill writes :—

"Sidney is very busy now about the Y.M.C.A. new building. He is in committee day after day about it. He will be glad when it is all over, as he has so much responsibility with regard to it all."

"*December* 4*th*.

"The Rev. H. Langley, from Melbourne, has been with us during the last three weeks. We were so sorry to lose him. He had a most successful mission at the Y.M.C.A. A large number of people were greatly helped, and many really converted to God. Sidney has not been so overworked lately. He superintended everything in regard to the Y.M.C.A. building itself. He bought all the furniture, sent to England for the linoleum, and to Sydney for the tesselated pavement. It all proved a success—furnishing and everything. Every one was pleased with the entire building. The Y.W.C.A. have taken an entire floor, for which they pay £84 a year. The girls are delighted, and we have over a hundred of them in to lunch every day. Sidney lets them go up to the gymnasium and have games."

The visit to Australia which we have recorded above resulted in an urgent request from the Bishop of Ballarat to take charge of an important parish in that city. The negotiation had to be done by cablegram, and left Mr. Hill very little time for reflection. Many things pointed towards acceptance. Ballarat is a very healthy city, standing high, with a much colder and more bracing climate than Auckland. The concentration of work would have been in some ways a rest to him, for his ardent temperament led him to take an active part in everything in Auckland that came in his way and awakened his interest, and the pressure on all sides was sometimes more than his strength could bear. Earnestly and solemnly the little family laid the matter before the Lord. Only to know and then to do His will was ever their one aim. The result was that the offer was rejected. " He felt he could not honourably leave all the work he has here and his friends so very suddenly." This is his wife's sole comment on the decision. No thought of worldly advantage or consideration for their own weal ever seems to have swayed their judgment for a moment. Honour was as strong a principle with Joseph Hill as with any knight of old. Commoner though he was, *noblesse oblige* was the motto of his life.

Bishop Thornton renewed the attack a little later, but without success. In the beginning of 1887 Mr. Hill was much tried by a sad event in connection with his prison work. It is so interesting that it will be given in detail in the next chapter. A change of thought and scene became necessary, and the whole party moved to Tauranga, where the Bishop had lent them his house.

"While here," writes Mrs. Hill, "Mr. Goodyear came and took us all to Maketu for a week. It was so amusing to be amongst the natives once more, and there are so many there. There was a large meeting and feasting of Hauhaus while we were there; *they* are not friendly to Europeans. (The Hauhaus fell back from Christianity, and have a sort of mixed religion, in some respects akin to Mahometanism.) Sidney went to them every day, and one day he put up his large Tabernacle pictures in their chief whare, and invited them to come and hear them explained. They came till the whare was packed, but they did not like it, and after listening for about half an hour, more than half of them got up and went out. It was such a singular scene, as very few had on English clothes, and twenty or thirty were lying full length on the ground asleep, or pretending to be."

Only once more did Mr. Hill visit his Maori friends, and of that last visit in 1889 we have no special record.

CHAPTER VI

WORK IN AUCKLAND (*Continued*)

"*It is best indeed*
To spend ourselves upon the general good;
And oft misunderstood,
To strive to lift the knees and limbs that bleed;
This is the best, the fullest meed.
Let ignorance assail or hatred sneer,
Who loves his race he shall not fear;
He suffers not for long,
Who doth his soul possess in loving, and grows strong."

LEWIS MORRIS.

CHAPTER VI

WORK IN AUCKLAND (Continued)

NO record of J. S. Hill's work in Auckland would be complete without some account of the marvellous blessing vouchsafed to his labours in the prison. We have seen how he began work there when first he came to New Zealand, and he gladly resumed it on his return to Auckland when he became Prison Chaplain. It is matter for sincere regret that there is no account of his ministrations. There was no branch of the Master's service for which he was better fitted. The absence of all conventionality, the Christ-like love for sinners, the absolute faith in his message and reality in delivering it, the sympathy and brotherliness of his manner, which overflowed his kind eyes and rang out in every word of his tender voice—all these things specially qualified him to deal with the outcasts of society. The most degraded know a true man when they see him, and as such the Auckland prisoners recognised and trusted him. The work he did in the gaol was solid work. No sham repentances passed muster with him. Though endued with the charity that "believeth all things," he was gifted too with a discerning of spirits which enabled him to detect hypocrisy and unmask deceit. In all branches of mission work, and among all classes, his special power as a physician of souls lay in the fact that he never healed a spiritual hurt slightly. There were those who thought him too severe and uncompromising; he was never accused of superficiality. To him sin was SIN, whether in the fashionable young lady or in the criminal under sentence of death. Sin must be acknowledged and dealt with before the message of pardon and peace could be offered. In a corrupt society he preached scathingly against the besetting sins of the community; in a prison, where wrong-doing was already reaping its reward, he could afford to be more compassionate. The character in fiction of which he most reminded one was Mr. Eden in "Never Too Late to Mend." The persistent running to earth of evil-doing, with indifference to personal consequences, so well described in the elder man, were as conspicuous in Mr. Hill as was his brotherly love. The blessing of his ministrations was not confined to the prisoners, but the gaolers shared it; more than one has reason to thank God for his memory. The following touching story may serve as a sample of many others written otherwise. It was taken down from his own lips, and if in any way it contradicts the current accounts, we would observe that it was his view, founded on the confessions of the prisoners, and is not intended in any way to reflect on the conclusions of judge and jury, acting on outside evidence.

C—— was mate of a vessel which traded between Auckland and the neighbouring islands. On one of these there lived a man with his family, for whom C—— used to do commissions, bringing him stores, etc. The poor lad became engaged to this man's daughter, and she came over from her island home to Auckland to be married; but just before the wedding she eloped with another man. After a time her lover deserted her, and C——, who was devotedly attached to her, followed her to her home, to which he heard she had returned. He forgave her, and again the day was fixed for their marriage. But either the girl was thoroughly unprincipled or the victim of some designing villain, for again and again she was missing, and at last C—— lost patience, and, priming himself with drink, went out swearing to get her. He got into a row with a policeman and knocked him down, for which he was sentenced to three months' imprisonment. While he was working out this punishment the girl he loved married another man. Then the tragedy began in earnest. C—— made a plot with the assistance of his friend P——, a larrikin lad of the same stamp, to carry off the girl to South America. They stocked their boat with provisions for some time, each man took a revolver and a rope, and then they landed on the island. One was to cover the girl with a pistol, the other to seize and carry her off. But, unfortunately, as they approached the father saw them, and noticed that C—— was carrying a revolver. Taking it for granted that he had come for revenge, he seized the intruder by the throat. P——, anxious about his friend, fired into the air to frighten him; but finding it had no effect he fired again, this time hitting him on the cheek and causing a great flow of blood. This caused him to loose his hold on C——, and seeing him drop the foolish young fellow concluded he was killed, and finished his deadly work with yet another shot. Then both turned to look for the girl, but she had escaped into the scrub through a window, so they returned to the boat and set sail for Sydney. Arrived there they went up-country, and might have escaped altogether, but they were both so miserable that they gave themselves up. One policeman, unarmed, brought them forty miles, they still carrying their revolvers. And so they were conducted back to Auckland for their trial. P—— pleaded not guilty by the advice of his lawyer. C—— said nothing, though he might have incriminated his companion. There was a lot of counter-swearing, and in the end both were condemned to death. It was at this stage that Mr. Hill, as Prison Chaplain, went to visit them.

"He could get nothing out of C——, who was an utterly ignorant man, without any knowledge whatever of the most elementary truths. P—— was different; he had been in a Church Sunday School, and was tolerably well taught. 'He grinned all over,' as the Chaplain graphically described it, and was quite defiant. 'I read the 32nd Psalm to him, and spoke of the necessity of confession and the blessing of forgiveness. Then I asked him if he knew the Lord's Prayer. "Oh, yes!" "Will you say it?" No, he couldn't do that. I said, "Then I will pray for you." I knelt and prayed. As I finished, before I could get up, he threw his arms round my neck and cried, "I killed T——." Struggling with my emotion, I said, "Will you tell C—— that?" "Oh no, you tell him." I said a little about the necessity of confession, and then I fetched C——. The two young men fell into one another's arms and sobbed like children. They had not spoken to one another since P—— had pleaded not guilty. The lawyers had pitted one against the other, each wanting, of course, to get his client off, and had saved neither. From that day I began to visit them daily, spending the whole morning with them. I had to begin at the very beginning with C——, who scarcely knew the name of Jesus, and nothing of His story. I told him the history of the Bible simply, a little more from day to day, leaving him a chapter to read and think about, such as Luke xv. One day I had been explaining the sacrifices pointing to Christ. The next morning he met me with "I can't get hold of the meaning of those sacrifices, sir, at all." So I fetched in White's book (on the Tabernacle), and showed him the pictures, especially the scapegoat. "Leave me this book," he said. The following day I found that the two prisoners, two warders, and the head gaoler had spent the whole night in his cell reading. All were in tears. They met me with "Jesus was the Lamb of God!"'"

From that time the growth in grace was marvellous. Mr. Hill, at their request, went to see the widow of the murdered man, and ask her forgiveness. The execution was indeed a touching scene. There was not a dry eye. Mr. Hill repeated the hymn "Jesu, Lover of my soul," as they walked calmly and firmly by his side to the scaffold, and after their faces were covered he heard them repeating it. Poor P——'s last words, as he grasped the hand of the man who had brought light and peace to him, were: "Mr. Hill, when you cross over there will, at all events, be one man watching for you on the other side."

This story is only one instance of the influence for good exerted by this faithful servant over the worst of criminals. And he strove also for their best temporal interests. He found that the letters from prisoners always went out with the gaol mark upon them. This of course was very prejudicial to the relatives, who must have felt the obloquy of having the disgrace of husband or son thus made public. Mr. Hill brought up this subject in his usual vigorous style when lecturing on the "Administration of Justice." His remarks were telegraphed to Wellington when the House was sitting. A member brought the subject forward, with the result that the practice was at once altered.

He was also intensely interested in the treatment of juvenile offenders, and never ceased to inveigh against the arrangement whereby children under ten were confined with hardened criminals. In his farewell address, when he was responding to the kind and complimentary remarks of the Aucklanders, he brought forward this subject again, and urged it on the citizens as a matter demanding prompt reform.

We do not know whether his burning words led to any change in the law.

Hospitality in the Colonies is apt to be imposed upon, and the Hills did not escape the deception often practised on kind-hearted people. There was one flagrant case of a young man who came to them from Napier, where he had been generously entertained. He said he was on the look-out for a situation, but in the meantime was starving. The best the house afforded was of course put before him, but he did not appear to have much appetite. The next day brought the landlord of one of the hotels with two cheques, one of which purported to be signed by Mr. Hill, the other by the Bishop of Waiapu. Needless to say, both were forgeries. He was sentenced to twelve months' imprisonment, of which Mr. Hill made good use, and there is reason to hope that he eventually started on a fresh life. The curious thing about the story was that this young man warned his hosts at Napier of a lady, also a stranger from England, staying in their house, denouncing her as an impostor, in which he proved the truth of the adage, "Set a thief to catch a thief," for his opinion was a correct one.

In May 1887 the Earl and Countess of Aberdeen paid a visit to Auckland, and gave, at Mr. Hill's request, addresses to the young men and young women respectively. Lord Aberdeen also gave what was characterised as "a splendid address" at the theatre service on Sunday night. Their sympathy and interest were a source of cheer to the busy workers. Mr. Hill found that, as a leader of thought, he was obliged to grapple with the politics of the Colony; but this was never to advance party interests, but to keep public opinion straight on moral points. Infidelity had penetrated to high places, and, as a general election was pending, it was a critical moment for the upholders of truth. The working-men were getting to repose such confidence in him that they sent him a deputation to ask if he would represent them in Parliament!

In the meantime he kept up the interest of the young people in physical development; and, acting on the old adage that example is better than precept, joined their football on Saturday afternoon. The following amusing comment is perhaps worth insertion:—

"A clergyman and a footballer are not frequently discovered to be one and the same individual, and it was with some measure of surprise, and also of pleasure, I must admit, that on Saturday afternoon last I came across a representative of the pulpit actively engaged in a football match. Probably there is only one person in Auckland who would have placed himself in such a position—and more's the pity—and the 'reverend' gentleman in question is the Rev. J. S. Hill. He has done a heap of good for the young men of Auckland by associating with them in whatever they may desire to engage in, so long as it is morally right and physically useful, and his entrance into the football field has already had excellent results. He has inaugurated the 'Association' game to take the place of the rough-and-tumble 'Rugby,' and the effect is much appreciated by all who have witnessed the new club matches. The 'Association' game, as played by the Rev. Mr. Hill's club and the warehousemen, was most orderly throughout, and I did not hear a cross word or an improper expression used from first to last. And there was Mr. Hill right in the thick of it, actually as enthusiastic as the most youthful of those engaged in the match, dressed in his white cricketing shirt, white knickers, and black stockings and shoes, watching every movement, kicking, dodging, and running, and evidently making thorough enjoyment for himself as well as for others. And he had to preach on the following day—for it was the Sabbath—and he did; and he preached well too, and he had none the fewer listeners because he had played a good game of football on the Saturday afternoon. Now, I want to suggest that the Rev. Mr. Hill should extend his praiseworthy operations, and get some of his long-faced brethren of the pulpit out in the field occasionally; for it would do them a world of good, and probably give their sermons a more effective force than ever was known before."

The writer of this letter forgot perhaps that Mr. Hill was President of the Y.M.C.A., and in that capacity felt himself bound to direct the sports of the young men—an obligation not certainly laid equally on all clergymen—but it was one of the things that made him powerful for good in Auckland, and therefore in his case to be commended, though not indiscriminately imitated.

Another visit to Australia in 1888 is thus chronicled by Mrs. Hill:—

"S—— and M—— left on April 10th for Sydney.

Splendid weather all the way. I feel so dull without them, but oh what an intense comfort to know that our Father-God orders all things for us! I have a dear friend staying with me. . . .

"The mission at Ballarat was very encouraging. When they returned to Melbourne the Sydney Y.M.C.A. wired to him to ask him to take a mission there for ten days, beginning May 11th; so he went, leaving M—— in Melbourne. I have just had letters from Sydney telling me the mission there was most encouraging, more so even than the one in Ballarat. On one evening large numbers of men received blessing, and many came to him saying that they had been blessed in attending his Bible class in Auckland; he wrote overflowing with joy. They are leaving Melbourne to-morrow or Wednesday for the Bluff, where they are due on the 29th. He will begin at once a mission at Dunedin."

This beautiful city contains a large Scotch colony, hard-headed practical men. The Prestyterian element is very strong. Christian work of all kinds is energetically carried on, but somewhat in grooves. Just the place which needed and would profit by such a shaking as Mr. Hill's preaching would give it.

We do not often insert newspaper comments, but the following just embodies the essence of his mission preaching:—

"We are at present enjoying a visit from the earnest evangelist the Rev. J. S. Hill, from Auckland. Mr. Hill speaks with great plainness and simplicity; his clear voice and pleading pathos in telling the story of God's love to man secure for him a willing ear and an anxious heart in his audiences. He speaks as one who is full of his momentous yet joyous message from God to man. At the outset of his addresses he sets up the mental picture of Jesus the Saviour of sinners, and never permits the eyes to wander away from the sacrificial Victim. He tells Christians that what they want is not so much 'more faith' as 'more fact.' They want more of the facts of Jesus; and while he keeps those facts ever issuing from a heart full of their power, he convinces sinners of the importance of those facts for their eternal salvation. The meetings which have been held have proved rich in Divine blessing to God's people, and the power of the Spirit is evident among those who formerly were indifferent to the Gospel news."

Once more the busy routine began at Auckland. At this time Mr. Hill was holding five services on Sunday. He began with the Prison at 9 a.m. Then morning service at a little church at the suburb of Remuera, the charge of which gave him an ecclesiastical status while he freely carried on his evangelistic and other labours. The men's Bible class was at three. At that time he was taking evening service at a town church, and the day's work concluded with the theatre at eight.

But work was his element. He was perfectly satisfied so long as he could see signs that it was owned of God.

"My own darling mother," he writes in September, "my work just now is most encouraging. The mission to Sydney and Ballarat was a very successful one; then returning South we had a grand work at Dunedin. Next month I am going to Nelson and Blenheim. Pastor Muller has been here; he is a fine specimen of a thorough Christian man, and his life's testimony is most useful in a place like this. I believe all the signs of the coming again of Christ are manifesting themselves. The constant rumours of wars, the earthquakes, the failing of men's hearts because of fear, and in thousands of ways it seems to me the world is fast ripening for the coming end of the dispensation.

" . . . My stay here is very uncertain, and before long I think we must try and get back to England, but the climate might not suit the little darlings."

Almost immediately after writing these last words which betray the father's heart, during his absence at Blenheim, the "little darlings" were attacked by scarlet fever. Then followed the news of the Rev. F. J. Leachman's death, so it was a sad time for Mrs. Hill and her sister. The longing for home began to be intensely felt, and no doubt expressed, as a rumour soon spread that they were going away. One lady lay awake all night after she heard it, another went so far as to pray that something might happen to prevent it, and there was real distress among their countless friends at the prospect of losing them. However, they could not let their house, so for the time the matter dropped.

A time of mutual cheer resulted from the visit of a lady from the old country in connection with the Y.W.C.A. She held a week's mission among the young women, and, though the weather was bad, the attendance kept up well, and much spiritual result followed and a life-long friendship.

Very pleasant are the memories of this glimpse at the busy happy home-life in Park Avenue. Mr. Hill had collected a large library; he was a man who appreciated books in the fullest sense of the word. He read and assimilated quickly, and the pleasure of getting a new listener who shared his passion was very great. He would often bring a volume of Westcott to table, and read passage after passage that delighted him, sometimes to the despair of his womenfolk.

One night at the little suburban church where he was then officiating he gave out the Communion hymn, "And now, O Father," after the service. As he was walking home with his friend, she asked him why he chose it when there was no celebration. "Oh," he exclaimed, in his eager way, "it is my *favourite* hymn; it is always spiritually true!"

Yes, to him the presence of the Lord was an abiding reality.

In November the Government sent a telegram to Mr. Hill, asking him to sit on a Commission to inquire into the sweating system of New Zealand. It may seem strange to English people that there should be such an evil in a young Colony, but, alas! the abuses of civilisation spread faster than its blessings. It was a kind of work for which Mr. Hill was eminently fitted. He was very quick at tracking out whatever he wanted to know; he would have thrown himself heart and soul and strength into any enterprise which promised deliverance to the oppressed. The terms offered were liberal; but no consideration would move him to fall short in the work he had undertaken, and finding the two incompatible, he reluctantly declined the honour.

So for a few months more the round of work went on. "Sidney works like a galley slave," says his wife.

The Pillar of Cloud lifted before a breakdown came.

All arrangements having been satisfactorily made, passage was taken on the *Mariposa*, which was to leave Auckland on March 24th, 1890, for San Francisco; the journey through America being chosen on account of relatives there whom they wished to visit. Besides this inducement, Mr. Hill wished to visit American prisons, in which he was facilitated by the kind offices of the New Zealand Government.

Nothing now remained but farewells, and these were no light matter in this case. Mr. and Mrs. Hill were not leaving one congregation. They were in a unique position. They belonged to the whole city, and it is no exaggeration to say that the whole city mourned at their departure. However, so convinced were the Aucklanders that Mr. Hill had become one of themselves, that they cherished more than hope that he would return. They let him go, laden with their blessings, wafted by their prayers, but it was on furlough. Warm and affectionate addresses flowed in from all classes—the

Church of England clergy, the Ministers' Association, the Young Men's Christian Association, and the prisoners at the gaol, the last a touching testimony to one who had ever acted on the beautiful motto of the saintly Dr. Guépin, "Aux plus déshérités, le plus d'amour."

At the representative farewell meeting at the City Hall, the following testimony, among many others, was given to the prison work by Archdeacon Dudley :—

"As in other departments," the speaker said, "he had done his work thoroughly in connection with the Mount Eden Gaol. He had spoken so plainly to the prisoners that their hearts quailed within them, and yet there was not one of them that did not love him. He (the speaker) had had a visit from three officers of that institution with a very respectable sum of money as a contribution to the testimonial to be presented to their friend. One of these officers said Mr. Hill had lightened their labours immensely by making the prisoners more amenable to discipline. *He had diminished crime in the gaol to an enormous extent.* Only those who knew what prisoners were knew what an amount of personal and social sin could be perpetrated in an institution of that kind. These officers testified that with God's blessing the prisoners were profoundly affected, and altogether changed in general demeanour, language, and spirit through Mr. Hill's influence."

Among the public comments on his career the following remarks from an outsider are much to the point :—

"He took up an exposed position from the first. He did not entrench himself in the pulpit, and content himself with being merely orthodox. He saw that the working classes, comprising many thoughtful men, did not attend the regular services of the Church. There are far more deep-thinking men amongst the best of our operative classes than amongst the class socially above them—the shopkeeping and mercantile class; and yet these intelligent working-men seldom go to church. Mr. Hill saw this, and he has done something to bring them back. He has honestly striven to follow them up; he has studied the questions which they study, and has entered into everything which interested them."

So the last day came, and a crowd accompanied them to the ship. The purser remarked, "There couldn't have been more to see the Prince of Wales off!" but to our mind it was more like the beloved Apostle's departure from Tyre. As the steamer put off from shore the hymn arose, "God be with you till we meet again," but it was broken by the sobs of the singers. One chapter of life's work was closed. Little did any of those who mourned the removal of their friend and teacher to another sphere of labour realise the full significance of those words "till we meet again." They hoped for and confidently expected an earthly reunion. In four short years the news was flashed to that shore, "*Bishop and Mrs. Hill dead.*" Then indeed was there lamentation. He had left them in such health and strength, with such fair promise of coming years. Could it be that that active brain was stilled for ever, that that loving heart had ceased to beat?

The valued General Secretary of the Y.M.C.A., Mr. Brakenrig, writes :—

"The news caused a profound sensation in Auckland ; the place was stirred as one never saw it before. Passing up Queen Street, I was stopped continually by those one little thought had been influenced by our beloved brother's words. A constable came to me with tears running down his cheeks : 'Can it be true, sir, the sad news we read in the paper? I cannot tell you what I owe to him ; he led me to the Saviour.' You will understand so well the earnest inquiries made to me, by all sorts of people, knowing how much one was connected with the beloved one when he laboured so devotedly here. . . . Many who to our eyes have been careless and indifferent have shown that the good seed of the Kingdom had been received through the loving, earnest words of our beloved friends when here, and much blessed fruit will yet be borne to the praise and glory of the Master's name."

The work of the Holy Ghost in human souls is so sacred a theme that one shrinks from saying much about it ; yet in closing the work of our brother in Auckland it may be well to give one or two instances of what is meant by the "blessing" which is so often spoken of as the result of his missions. He aimed simply and directly at bringing souls into contact with a personal, living Saviour. Some words of his own in an invitation letter to a children's mission are so apposite that they may well be quoted here :—

"In one of our cathedrals there is a beautiful piece of work in which some one is holding up the wounded hand of Jesus. I just desire to do that, and we do pray that you will place your hand in His, and let Him from this mission time henceforth lead you."

Here are a few sentences from a letter received from one who had heard his preaching in Auckland :—

"God Almighty bless you. If it is any satisfaction to you—and I am sure it is—you have been the instrument in God's hand of bringing me to the foot of the Cross. Oh ! the love I bear to you, next my Saviour, no one can tell. . . . I pray for you night and morning. I should like to speak with you, and shake you by the hand, and thank you personally. . . . Thanks be to God, I have found my Jesus, and you have been the instrument."

There is a simplicity and ring of reality about this letter that could not fail to strike the most prejudiced, and it is only a specimen of those which God's honoured servant was privileged to receive. To one of his mission services came from curiosity a lady in an influential position in her neighbourhood, fond of races, balls, and all devices to kill time, but utterly ignorant of the claims of God. She was interested, and when a mission began near her home, she resolved to attend it. One night Mr. Hill was aroused from his sleep by a request to go and see what help he could give to a distressed soul. Her husband had sat up with her till four o'clock, both of them searching the Bible and trying to find how they might "get right with God." Unable to calm her, he had sent for the mission preacher three miles off. "He of course went at once, and after praying with them both, he explained the glorious Gospel once more, and it pleased God before daylight to give her a full deep joy, . . . resting on Christ so simply."

This lady's testimony among her friends was used by God to His glory in them also.

Another deeply interesting instance of the blessing attending his preaching is found in the case of a young man who saw him first when he landed from the steamer which was wrecked near Tauranga. He was pointed out to him as the "plucky parson" who, with one of the ship's cabin boys, had, at considerable personal risk, succeeded in saving much of the passengers' luggage.

"I was," he says, "at this time principally struck by his extreme activity and his utter forgetfulness of self. While others were knocked up with spending several hours on the rocks in the sun, and then several more hours cramped up in the ship's boats, this young clergyman bounded about looking after his own and others' property, as only a real athlete can do. . . . The more I got to know him, the more strong did his influence over me become. A Gospel address on John vi. 37, 'Him that cometh unto Me I will in no wise cast out,' decided me. I wrote to the Bishop and told him that under God he had been the means of my conversion to God. He was then just starting on a mission to the South Island and Australia, and probably got my letter as he went on board the steamer. I shall never forget my first meeting with him on his return. Such meetings are too personal, too sacred, to put down on paper."

This young man followed him into the mission field. Bishop Stuart remarks that he was constantly meeting with men who had, in a similar manner, received a message of life from his lips.

One cannot help lingering over the loving reminiscences of such a life of constant testimony and service. There were with him no business hours. He was *always* on duty. He would over and over again leave a meal out of his day to rush down to the wharf just to say good-bye to some poor creature out of gaol for whom he had obtained a passage to another Colony, where he could begin life afresh.

Afterwards, when going to Africa, a quartermaster came up and saluted the Bishop. Some of the party began questioning the man as to where he had met Dr. Hill, but the latter stopped them, saying, "Surely I've knocked about the world enough for this man to have rubbed up against me somewhere." Afterwards the Bishop explained, "with a merry twinkle in his eye," that their last meeting had been outside Auckland Gaol.

One striking incident, illustrating how closely he kept to his heavenly Master, will fitly close this chapter.

When in Poverty Bay he became acquainted with a man who had a run in the neighbourhood, and who bore an exceedingly bad character. He was on one occasion strongly impressed with a feeling that he must go and see this man, whom we will call K——. It was Saturday morning, and he was preparing his sermon for Sunday. He tried to collect his thoughts, but again and again the impression returned, Go and see K——. At last he felt it was the voice of God, and he went and told his wife. She asked in some surprise, "What are you going to see that man for?" He could not tell, he was being sent. On the way he called on his friend Mr. A. B——, and found his horse saddled at the door. When Mr. Hill explained to his friend that he wanted his company on his errand, to the astonishment of both it came out that the same impression had been on Mr. A. B——'s mind, to the extent that he had saddled his horse, intending to ride over.

They found K—— at home, and had a long and earnest talk with him. At first he listened quietly, but afterwards grew angry and almost drove them from his house. The messengers of mercy returned sadly enough, yet conscious that they had done their duty.

That night K——, riding home half-drunk, was thrown from his horse, and taken up dead! How solemnly this story illustrates the words of the Prophet: "If thou warn the wicked, and he turn not from his wickedness, nor from his wicked way, he shall die in his iniquity; but thou hast delivered thy soul."

CHAPTER VII

HOME MISSION WORK

"*Blending their souls' sublimest needs*
With tasks of every day,
They went about their gravest deeds
As noble boys at play."—LORD HOUGHTON.

CHAPTER VII

HOME MISSION WORK

"San Francisco,
"*April* 1890.

"WE landed here April 16th. The night before was so rough that I hardly expected we should. The ship had not enough cargo on, and the consequence was that in the gale she rolled most heavily, and kept on shipping seas so much that they had trouble to keep the engine-fires alight. However, here we are in a most comfortable hotel. It is a most irreligious place. On Sunday all the theatres and most of the shops are open, and the people go by tram and train to the park, where a splendid band plays. But what to my mind is worst of all is that all the churches and chapels have *secular* lectures at the Sunday evening services, to try and attract the people, as well as paid singers, and wind instruments are used at some of the services.

"Travelling through America will be good for S., and he will make good use of it. He has gone now to visit the prison. . . ."

We could wish that the travellers had recorded their impressions of Salt Lake City, where they stayed two days, but we have only a rapid itinerary, showing that they stayed a night or two *en route* all the way, extending it to a week at Denver, till they reached New York, where they remained three weeks, finally embarking for home on the S.S. *Servia.*

One can imagine the joyful return after twelve years' absence, chastened as it necessarily was by finding some vacant places in the circle of relations and friends. But Joseph Hill had his mother still, and to her he hastened. For some time the family made Brighton, where she joined them, their head-quarters. But rest did not mean idleness, and in December of the same year Mr. Hill began mission work in connection with the Rev. W. Hay Aitken, in the Church Parochial Mission Society. It was a most happy time ; he was thoroughly in his element. He was a successful missioner in the best and fullest sense of the word. He had no stereotyped methods in after meetings, and was always willing to adopt suggestions even from his workers. He could never do anything in a crowded inquiry room, and always tried to get a perfectly quiet place in which to deal with an anxious soul. It has already been noticed that he was singularly gifted with discerning of spirits. Sometimes he would pass from one to another in a church and set them praying, but would not stop and talk to any till he was fully convinced that the right moment had come, and then he would stay any length of time. The girls he would always turn over to the lady workers. His addresses delivered at weekly celebrations during a mission were profoundly beautiful, one may say unequalled for intense spirituality and lofty aim. But his fulness of thought often obscured his meaning, and led to a paradoxical style, which was occasionally misunderstood. Though not a student of poetry, there was a poetical side to his mind, which helped him much (as it always helps) in dealing with mere party questions. He liked to look round a question, and the result was, on disputed points, a grand tolerance and a little vagueness. Firmly rooted in the great foundation truths of the Faith, he could afford to sympathise with many who held widely divergent views on minor points. Sympathy was with him nothing less than a passion, and he loved to find an answering chord in a dead writer as in a living friend. His education had been deficient on the imaginative side, and his life had been too sternly practical. When once urged by an enthusiastic friend to the study of Browning, he laughed, and said life was too short for poetry. Yet at that time he was tearing through (no other expression so well conveys his reading) every treatise on ethics which came across him. He was very fond of talking out a subject which interested him, especially at night, and could never be got to see the necessity of going to bed! He had to be driven to his rest. When he got a listener who really understood him, he unlocked his innermost heart. He was no longer practical; one learnt the mystical side of his nature. But this never came out except to one who could enter into it.

During this period of direct mission work, while he was engaged in what he loved best and was most successful in, his mind was being drawn in a remarkable way back to the mission field. The coming of the Lord largely occupied his thoughts, and the need to be up and doing continually pressed him forward. In an earnest conversation with a few intimate friends at Keswick, in August 1891, he tried to express his views on the evangelisation of the world. He did not agree with the self-reproach with which some Christians regard the history of foreign missions, blaming the Church for her inaction during the centuries between the evangelisation of Europe and the inauguration of the modern movement. He loved rather to see the Divine Government at work in times and seasons, and to watch with solemn joy the unlocking of door after door for the messengers of Christ to go and possess the lands of His inheritance. He felt that the modern preaching of a mission crusade laid too much stress on human effort and made too little account of the Divine purposes. He deprecated the rush to the mission field of untrained, inexperienced workers, acting on the mere cry that "the heathen are perishing." We who knew his enthusiastic nature were a little startled at what seemed like a change of view, but there was no ground for fear. He was only working his way towards a clear reason for laying down his life. He who was so impulsive was resolved that the sacrifice should be laid upon no mere impulse, but upon a solemn conviction; and that conviction was given to him. When he offered himself for Africa it was because he believed that God wanted him there, because he saw clearly that that great continent was being given bit by bit into English hands for Christ's own great purpose of salvation.

The story of the West Coast, with all its quenched efforts, its martyrs' graves, was to him a solemn inspiration. Underneath it all, too, came the voice of his early youth, calling him back to the land of his first choice. Very dear to him was the Society that had trained and sent him forth. He felt his God-given power to grapple with difficulties, to unite by the display and exercise of love discordant elements.

And with his conscious, ever-deepening, ever-intensified personal sense of Pardoning Grace grew the memory, so early stamped on his heart, of the awful nameless sins of heathendom. To him they were not the taint of savage nature, they were affronts to the holiness and forbearance of God. He could never grow accustomed to devil worship, with all its lustful horrors. The degradation of ignorance did not only awaken in him pity and helpfulness, it bowed him like a prophet of old in agony of soul before His outraged Lord.

After his acceptance by the Church Missionary Society he preached as never before, with an eager longing to provoke interest in the languid souls of prosperous, respectable, easy-going Christians in winning Africa for Christ.

The Hills were then living in Park Lane, Stoke Newington. Immediately opposite their house was the garden of the "Willows," the well-known training home of the missionary candidates of C.M.S., Zenana, and other Societies, and also of Mildmay Deaconesses. Mr. Hill was deeply attached to Mrs. Pennefather, the beloved foundress and head of the extensive work carried on at Mildmay Park, and he had dear and intimate friends in that busy hive, so that there was seldom a day when he was at home that he did not pass through the "Compound," as the enclosure containing the various institutions is familiarly called. Occasionally, too, his voice was heard in the large Conference Hall in Sunday evening evangelistic services. But he was not often suffered to remain at home. So many were his engagements that he often spent his nights in the train. Then came the Committees, fraught with intense interest to the little home circle, as appears in the following letter by Mrs. Hill:—

"From February 8th to the 22nd he was at Guildford, assisting Mr. Aitken. From March 1st to 15th at Streatham Common. From the 22nd to 29th at Fairlight (near Hastings), where he was over a fortnight, and where I stayed also from the Thursday week. It was wet every day, and yet the mission, I am sure, was far from a failure; in fact the Vicar and his wife were greatly cheered by it. There is no village, and all the parishioners are scattered about, but the Vicar used to send a large waggon to fetch the old and infirm up to the services. The whole family did all they could to make the mission a success, and I feel sure the results will be lasting. One of their own servants was converted during the time, and several other cases we heard of.

"But about Africa. He has to go before the Committee next Thursday at twelve, when his case will, I suppose, be settled. M—— is dreadfully down about it, as she says we are certain to be sent. Of course it is probable. At the same time I am certain if God sends us to Africa He will take care—of course He will—of my darlings; and though I cannot trust myself to think of the separation, I can trust Him with it all.

"When Sidney came home from Fairlight he had to go that same day to Maidstone, and home by one o'clock a.m. On April 7th he is going to Wolverhampton for a week, and the following Saturday to Bath for a fortnight. Since being at Fairlight he has been to Boston, where the kind and good Canon Blenkin cheered him up so much—not so much from the good he had himself been able to do, as from the good he received from the dear old man."

This was one of those seasons of Christian intercourse with men of higher scholarship and wider culture to which Bishop Hill always looked back with such pleasure. He constantly quoted Canon Blenkin, and when he met him for the last time at Keswick, it was with the feelings of a son, to judge by the warmth of the greeting. The elder saint preceded him to Paradise.

Of these missions the record is in heaven. Joseph Hill's powers as a missioner were not greater than many another who is labouring for God and souls in that most blessed "line of things." But those who knew and loved him, and many who only had the privilege of hearing him in the pulpit, will do more than pardon us for lingering over this part of his ministry—they will expect it of us.

A clergyman's wife, writing of a mission in her husband's parish, says :—

"Winning to Christ by his very loving manner, Mr. Hill was specially attractive to simple folk. As one said to me, 'You feel you can't help but be sorry for your sins, he speaks so lovingly.' Our servants would have done anything for him. *Whole households* of servants received memorial cards at the close of the mission."

This friend speaks of the beauty of his character in the home, "where his humility and gentleness shone very brightly." And she adds: "Independent testimony comes back to us from Lagos of the happy influence which he and Mrs. Hill had during their brief career among official circles there." It is often said of teachers it is as well not to know them too closely. The opposite is strictly true of Bishop Hill : the nearer one came to him, the better one loved and admired him. His faults were all on the surface ; he was sound to the core.

The Rev. W. Hay Aitken, writing of the time when Mr. Hill was his helper in mission work, says :—

"There was an air of intense reality about all his ministrations which impressed me very profoundly ; at the same time there was no constrained mannerism, no affectation of sanctimoniousness. No one could be brighter or more full of innocent mirth than he."

The time was now approaching for that solemn crisis in his life's work which was to bring him so soon to his rest.

Everybody has heard of the Nile Delta, but the Niger Delta is not such a familiar region ; yet it has played its part for a long time in Missionary history. Extending one hundred and twenty miles along the coast, the many towns on the river branches carry on a brisk trade in palm oil with the Royal Niger Company, which has factories and steamers for this purpose. Here Bishop Crowther established several mission stations, and as his diocese embraced the whole river, there was also work going on on the Lower and Upper Niger. It was only a year before his death that Mr. Graham Wilmot Brooke and the Rev. J. A. Robinson visited the Upper Niger Mission, and established themselves at Lokoja. But death and sickness soon broke up the little party of missionaries ; the leaders rest in the Africa for which they gave their lives, and the others returned home. After the death of the Bishop trouble arose, some of the Delta congregations separating themselves from the Church Missionary Society and forming what is known as the Niger Delta Pastorate. It became necessary to appoint a successor, and both in Africa and England there was a strong difference of opinion, some feeling that another African Bishop should be appointed, others convinced that a work that had proved too much for the supervision of an able man like Bishop Crowther was best, for the present, entrusted to an

Englishman. The difficulty was overcome by Joseph Hill, who had already been designated for that field as a missionary, being sent out as the Archbishop's Commissary and Bishop Designate in Western Equatorial Africa, with instructions to select two earnest and godly men to be consecrated with him as Assistant-Bishops. Naturally these arrangements took much time and thought, and he was continually in the committee room at Salisbury Square, until, after a period of anxiety and suspense to all concerned, we read :—

"Sidney has at last had an interview with the Archbishop of Canterbury, who is very strong indeed about having a native Bishop as well as an English one. . . . He proposes that Sidney should go very soon to have a look round and try and find two native men who could be consecrated with him as Assistant-Bishops, Sidney to be Bishop Designate until they can come to England, and all be consecrated together. Sidney is to submit the Archbishop's proposals to the C.M.S. Committee."

On July 23rd the Archbishop and the Bishop of London met Mr. Wigram at the House of Lords, and it was finally decided that Mr. Hill should go for six months as the Archbishop's Commissary. The delay was a relief to the Bishop Designate. He busied himself in working out his plans for the Niger Mission, and took a much needed rest at Keswick as the guest of Mr. and Mrs. Wigram.

Mrs. Hill writes, September 7th :—

"We leave Euston Square Station for Liverpool on Friday, at 10.5. The *Boma* sails at 10 o'clock on Saturday morning. The good-byes are to be said at Euston. Sidney is to spend a long evening with the Archbishop to-morrow; he very much wished him to stay a night or two, and wrote twice to that effect himself, but being so near the date of sailing Sidney felt he could not stay.

"He preached at Great Yarmouth on Sunday morning and evening, and that big church, the largest in England, was crammed. . . .

"He has had another interesting offer for the Niger from a lady at Mildmay. She prayed that if the Lord would have her go Sidney might speak to her personally about it, and he did *that very day.* I know you will think of us on Friday; it will be a bitter parting, and yet we have many great encouragements."

CHAPTER VIII

AFRICA AFTER SIXTEEN YEARS

"*A wealth of love and prayer behind,*
Far-reaching hope before,
The servants of the Lord go forth
To seek the foreign shore;
And wheresoe'er their footsteps move
That hope makes sweet the air;
And all the path is paved with love,
And canopied with prayer."

SARAH G. STOCK.

CHAPTER VIII

AFRICA AFTER SIXTEEN YEARS

"BAY OF BISCAY, *September* 13*th*, 1892.

"MY DARLINGS,—

"We are making straight for Grand Canary, where father hopes to meet Dr. Battersby, who is on his way home. You will be glad to hear that we are having a most lovely passage, which I cannot help putting down to a little sentence I heard a good many times before coming away, 'Please let them have a smooth passage.' Well, do you know, the old Biscay is more like a duckpond, only the very slightest roll, so that it is as enjoyable as a sea-life can be under the circumstances. This ship is a steady-going old thing, with none of the modern improvements—none of your electric light, but those little oil lamps, so that we were very glad of the nightlights father brought, which gave far more light and no smell. The food, too, is not of the best; yesterday we were several of us feeling queer, and the bill of fare was: salt boiled beef, roast pork and roast duck, and ox-tail stewed; then the sweets, rhubarb pie, cabinet pudding, and Banbury cakes! However, I have only missed one meal, and that was from being kept too long waiting. Our cabin is a particularly nice one, amidships. The port can be open in the roughest weather, because there is a passage-way beyond it, and this will be a *great* advantage in the tropics. The ship is not so big as the *Mariposa*, of immortal memory. We have twenty-six male passengers and four ladies altogether; but the saloon passengers are gentlemen, and very different from those who went out in the *Bonny* sixteen years ago. Most of the passengers leave the ship at Sierra Leone, but father is not quite decided whether he will stay there or go straight on to Lagos. . . .

"I hope all the rabbits and mice, tortoises and fowls, are well, and dear old Scipio, as well as Auntie's 'foxie.' It goes without saying that we think *so* much of you *all*, and wonder what you are doing."

Three days after one of the loving father's own letters was typewritten.

"S.S. 'BOMA,' JUST OFF GRAND CANARY,
"*September 16th*, 1892.

"MY SWEETEST, DARLING PETS,—

"So often have your brave yet pained and troubled little faces come to my mind, just as I saw them on leaving the station at Euston. Sometimes it is in the night, when I am not able to sleep, and then a vision of you all comes to me as I look into the deep blue sea when alone on deck. My poor heart has never had so great a trial as this sad parting from my loved ones at home. May the One who gave up all for us give to you and to us His blessed love to bind our hearts to His dear self, so that in Him we may feel we are never far away, but always near. I am quite sure you have both just put us into His loving arms to keep for you until we meet again, and in those arms we are safe, and so are you, my precious darlings.

"We have been to-day thinking of you going back to school, and wondering if you are going to try and be first as many times as last term, and if you will miss us quite as much when at your daily lessons. I remember a story of a little boy who used to say when he had anything very hard to do, 'Only a little at a time.' If it was raining he would say, 'Only a few drops at a time'; and if he had to cut up a large bundle of sticks he would say, 'Only a stick at a time,' and then the thing he had to do did not seem so hard. Could not you think of our being away as only a day at a time, and then it will so soon be gone? Now, my darlings, do all you can to make Auntie as happy as possible, and be good little girls, trying to please everybody, not forgetting the loving Lord Jesus. With our deepest love,

"Ever your loving old

"DAD."

The party arrived at Sierra Leone on September 23rd, where they were met by Dr. Harford-Battersby, who had remained behind on purpose to welcome them. They went to Bishopscourt, but Bishop Ingham was at that time absent. Mrs. Hill writes of the extreme loveliness of Sierra Leone seen in the early morning light. They were much delighted with the new Cottage Hospital—

"A really splendid building for the place, with two such nice nurses, dressed just like the Mildmay deaconesses, Miss Griffin and Sister Dorothy. They have a little meeting for the men who come for medicine every morning, at a quarter to eight, lasting about twenty minutes. Already so many poor Africans take advantage of the medical help that they are obliged to admit them by ticket, and after a certain number simply from want of time. It was a great boon to them to have Dr. Battersby, whom they have persuaded to stay another week."

Very refreshing after board ship were the comforts of Bishopscourt, and the black attendants delighted them with a grand display of flowers on the table—oleanders, roses, lovely white and scarlet lilies, and Cape jasmine. Humming birds and butterflies were in abundance, the latter so lovely and rare that specimens sometimes sell for five pounds.

A visit to the Annie Walsh Memorial School was a great refreshment to Mrs. Hill; only ladies who have known what it is to arrive weary in a foreign land after having been pent up on board a *not* first-class steamer can enter into the feeling with which she describes her visit:—

"The ladies there are so nice. The moment we arrived Miss Dunkley opened the door to us herself, and had afternoon tea in, and it was altogether quite a little taste of home. Their drawing-room was more like an English one than anything I have seen in Africa yet—all very simple, but so beautifully clean and tastily arranged, and the whole of the house was in keeping. After we had sat for some time and admired their view, verandah, trees, flowers, etc., we went into the schoolroom, where we found about fifty native girls, all very clean and tidy and bright-looking. Sidney gave them a short address, with several anecdotes, which they evidently appreciated."

Bishop Hill, as he was now called in Africa, preached three times at the cathedral,—aheavy day's work for the tropics. But it must have been inspiring to be preaching to thirteen hundred Africans, and to look down on that sea of black faces listening intently to the "old, old story."

But what a contrast to the decorous Sunday walk to church in England was the procession of old bath chairs, pulled and pushed by stalwart natives at their utmost speed—one nearly overturned in the gutter, others driven up against one another, all jolted and bumped abominably!

Yet Mrs. Hill has time to admire the little children, "mostly naked, or with a short skirt or handkerchief half covering their dear little shiny bodies." The Bishop had a kind of palanquin, but having tried it he preferred the bath chair!

Mrs. Hill gives such an interesting description of their further voyage that we give it as it stands in one of her circular letters.

"Our journey from Sierra Leone, which we left at 6 p.m. on Monday, has not been so pleasant as before. Owing probably to the damp heat, the meat and all the food on board is not nearly so good as it was, and from the large amount of cargo which was landed at Sierra Leone, Grand Bassam, and other places, the *Boma* is much higher out of the water, and rolls more. We have a large number of natives on board, chiefly 'Kru boys,' whom the Captain takes along the coast for any trader who needs native servants or labourers, and he gets 5*s*. per head for supplying them—a kind of Registry Office! They eat only rice twice a day; a good many are really boys about 12 or 14, and have such bright faces. I do so love African children.

But about 27 of the men work the ship. We have called at so many places since leaving Sierra Leone, for the *Boma* is like a big shop, and calls at the towns where they are in need of supplies of food or coal, which they can tell in a moment by flag signals. But at Cape Coast Castle, where the traders were expecting a heavy cargo, the Governor had ordered all vessels to be quarantined and nothing landed, so we had again, as at Grand Canary, to go through the farce of passengers and crew all being examined by a medical man sent on board for that purpose. Even so we were sent on to Accra, and have had to return here (Cape Coast Castle) again, which is a clear loss of 24 hours, and will prevent our getting to Lagos on Saturday. On Sunday morning early we were at Grand Bassam, where they landed 750 kegs of gunpowder; the crane working at it awoke me, and it gave me such an awful sense of shame that with *every* steamer (and they come along oftener than once a week, year in, year out) there is a practical denial of God in the cargoes they land of firearms, powder, rum, etc., and in the lives of the traders, who come by dozens in every ship, and are willing to risk their lives for *money*, while such a miserable few come along to give these poor natives the message of God's love to them. Sunday is the busiest day on board these steamers. We had only a tiny congregation last Sunday, because we called at another town and landed more powder. The Captain brought 2,000 kegs of it! They are landing goods all day, and nearly every day, and travel at night. The boats come out in dozens, each one with 12 natives paddling (6 each side) and one more to steer. The paddles they use are so like a bird's claw in shape, with three long talons, and they paddle with such precision, that it looks at a little distance just like one huge bird coming. Their only dress is a large handkerchief tied round the middle of the body, but their skins are so shiny, and being black, one does not notice the small amount of clothing. It is really wonderful that there are not many serious accidents in putting the cargo on the boats; for instance, dozens of heavy casks of coal, each a great weight, they send over the side of the *Boma* by the crane into these small boats with 13 natives in each, but the waves lift the boat up many feet, and then down again, and they have to guess just the right moment to let the cask drop, for it would be instant death if it fell on any man, even an African; but they are always on the alert, and jump overboard the moment there is danger. Often each day there are several natives swimming about to avoid the heavy casks and cases coming on their heads. Yesterday I saw three get a knock that I am sure would have injured an Englishman, but their skulls are thicker and their bodies very powerful. We have several native passengers in the saloon now—one who landed this morning was a very wealthy old gentleman with a number of servants. . . . They landed him by the crane in a basket—one of those numberless little absurd things that one sees in Africa that cause us to laugh almost to tears. He waved his mushroom hat as he was going down!

"QUETTAH, *October 7th*.

"The Captain tells us that we shall be in Lagos to-morrow; he is missing one or two ports in order to do so. . . . It will be so lovely to spend a quiet Sunday on shore. Quettah is famous for ducks, geese, and fowls, besides tomatoes, etc.; and the canoes have just come alongside and the natives scrambled up by dozens like monkeys, each carrying a heap of birds strung together on their shoulders, and are all clamouring round the chief steward and cook, who are purchasing. It seems a clean, lively little place; there are more people on the sandy shore than at any place we have called at, but it is a slave coast.

"C.M.S., LAGOS,
"*Monday, October 10th.*

"We landed about 1.30 on Saturday; a branch steamer came to the Lagos roads for us, as it is utterly unsafe for a small boat to cross the bar—and yet the ocean steamers cannot get in. The bar on Saturday was unusually smooth; I was so thankful for it, for it was not smooth at sea, and going from the *Boma* to the branch steamer in the little rowing boat, it was very rough. We were let down by the crane in arm-chairs; . . . it is a very uncomfortable experience, but only lasts about half a minute. On the bar there was a steamer that was wrecked on it two months ago; they cannot lift it or attempt to do so, because the bar is such a dangerous one. No lives were lost, for they had only recently subscribed for a life-boat, and she saved the sixty or more people on board. As we passed Christ Church here, Mr. Tugwell and Mr. Dods were waiting at the wharf, and soon Mr. Vernall came along; the ladies, four in number, met us at the house, and gave us a hearty welcome. Mr. Tugwell is the secretary here, and occupies the place and position old Mr. Maser had; but as he is an unmarried man, Mr. and Mrs. Dods are keeping house for him just now, and he boards with them *pro tem.*, as we are doing. You may remember seeing them dismissed about May from Salisbury Square. They were appointed to Abeokuta, but the way is blocked, and has been for some months, owing to some tribal war, so they cannot get in there, and for the same reason Mr. Buckley Wood cannot get away. Sidney had written to ask Mr. Wood to meet him here, but this is impossible. Mr. and Mrs. Vernall are at the

Training Institution just behind this house, and Miss Thomas and Miss Goodall are in charge of the Female Training Institution, which is just at the side of this mission house. . . .

"Sidney preached at Christ Church, which stands in the mission compound, yesterday morning, but the congregation had fallen off from what it was sixteen years ago. In the evening Mr. Dods preached, and in the afternoon Mr. Tugwell had a little service for children at four o'clock. Lagos has improved so very much since we were here in 1876 that I should hardly have recognised it. The township is far handsomer and the houses much better built than at Sierra Leone, but, of course, it lacks the lovely mountain scenery of the latter. . . . One little arrangement amuses me, which is that a little before six in the morning there is a knock at our bedroom door, and two boys come in, one a big boy, the other about twelve, and they sweep the room and put it straight just as a housemaid would do at eleven o'clock at home. Sidney makes use of the opportunity to learn a little Yoruba; he asks the names of everything they touch, and repeats it after them several times. They are such nice boys. There has one most encouraging incident just occurred: a chief from the interior has heard in some way of missionaries and their teaching, and he has come down to Lagos with a number of his people to learn all about it; he comes to every service or meeting of any kind that they have; he is such a tall fine man, with such a very intelligent face. He comes to the mission house very often, and is just now talking to Sidney; they get one of the house boys, of whom there are eight, to interpret. It seems to me so much more hopeful to try and teach a native of this stamp the Gospel, because they have not been demoralised by contact with Europeans, like the coast natives. There is not a European thread about this man: he has a flowing country cloth of bright yellow; a very big hat with broad brims and long streamers of several colours, tied up at both sides; a bracelet and necklace, all of African make. I need hardly say to some of you dear home-folks, Pray for him, for I am sure you will, and am equally—nay, more sure—that God will answer the prayer. One cheering piece of news we heard this morning, that the Babalao who was converted at Leke in 1877 and took the name at his baptism of Joseph Sidney is now a recognised teacher there, and, in fact, just now the only preacher they have, for Leke has been quite given up by all the Europeans; the traders have all left.

"We are having the most lovely weather. The rains are not over; the consequence is we have such a beautiful air, although, of course, it *is* warm, but the breeze is delightful. We are all in splendid health, and Sidney is just now surrounded by a company of natives, as well as the English missionaries, and is making them all laugh heartily, which indicates that he is not very depressed."

Meanwhile the work went on apace. Mrs. Hill was kept very busy typewriting for her husband, and learning Yoruba. Then Miss Goodall became ill, and Miss Warner went into the Female Institution to teach, while Mrs. Hill undertook the finishing-off of the needlework, in view of a Government Inspection.

There is many a warm mention of Mr. Tugwell (now Bishop) in the home letters, and he was a great comfort to Bishop Hill at that time.

The following account of their visit to Igannui, on the mainland, is so interesting that we will quote it *in extenso*. After waiting a long time past the appointed hour for their canoe, Mrs. Hill writes:—

"However we went, and we were most thankful we did so, for, besides spending a most pleasant day, Sidney and Mr. Dods had two or three opportunities of preaching the old, old story.

"After being in the canoe an hour and a half, we landed up such a pretty creek, where the wild flowers were so lovely. It was a good hour's walk to Igannui through the bush, and we passed such quantities of bananas, pine-apples, and cocoanuts growing wild, and also, what I had never seen before, the cocoa-tree, with the nuts on it nearly ripe. At Igannui Mr. Braithwaite, the African Catechist (who was at Leke when we were there in 1876-7) was expecting us, and had prepared a room where we could rest and dine—in fact he gave us possession of his house for the day. While we had breakfast (we had taken our own food, as these Africans are *very* poor) he rang the bell and gathered in his little church, which is also the schoolroom, a congregation of about sixty to seventy adults and thirty or more children.

"The building is of mud, thatched with palm-leaves, etc., but fairly solid, having however open sides instead of windows. Sidney gave the first address, telling them how his life had been saved by an African, and that he loved their people. They listened so intently while both he and Mr. Dods gave them the Gospel message, Mr. Braithwaite acting as interpreter—and a very good one he is. After the meeting was over, Mr. Dods, who had brought his camera, photographed some of them. It was a most amusing scene, for they nearly all wanted to be taken, though they did not understand it a bit; but Mr. Dods particularly wanted to photograph the church, only he could not get the people out of the way. Numbers of them wanted to look through under the velveteen cloth, which they did, and laughed so heartily when they found the people upside down. The children were *so* pretty, but they seemed to think they ought to be clothed before English visitors, and they pulled on old shirts, etc., which, being all in rags, did not look half so well as their natural clothing—their own ebony skins.

"While at Igannui I watched some babies being fed, and it is so peculiar, being universal through Africa. I will try to describe it. The mother lays the baby across her knees, with its head hanging over one side; she has beside her a calabash full of clean water, and a small one with the food in; it looked like very thin clear starch. She pours the food into her right hand, and, putting it under the baby's mouth, pours it down, and they are so used to the process that scarcely a drop is lost; then she shakes the baby's head to make sure it has swallowed it. Then she dips her hand into the clean water, and begins again. It was so extraordinary that I watched in utter astonishment. Baby sometimes kicks, screams, and resists, but all to no purpose: it is feeding-time, and the food must go down. Even the youngest baby has a bracelet on its wrist, and most of them wear necklaces or a string of beads round the body, and this is quite full-dress until they are eight or nine years old. Mrs. Dods (who is very pale and has a very white hand) induced a little black boy to shake hands with her; he cried with fright before he did it, and when it was done ran away, looking at his hand to see if the white came off!"

The hospitable people loaded them with fruit and a pair of fowls, and they went home, preaching on the way, and trying to reach the canoe-men, not able to bear the thought that those who toiled for their Christian visitors should be outside, alien to the commonwealth of God's people.

Shortly after Mrs. Hill had the anxiety of tending Miss Warner in her first attack of fever, but fortunately it passed off without bad results.

It is not our purpose in this brief memoir to give any account of the troublous times through which the Church in West Africa was now passing. It is enough to say that Bishop Hill went out with the confidence of the Archbishop and of the Society, and that he fully and admirably fulfilled his commission. His task was one of extreme difficulty, requiring the utmost delicacy and tact, but those sterling qualities which had characterised him all his life did not fail him when he needed them most. Truth and love were wonderfully blended in his character; he knew to a remarkable degree how to "be sincere in love." He never trimmed to please anybody, and so he succeeded in keeping the respect of all. Yet there were moments of depression, and in his report to the Archbishop he begs to be allowed to retire from the destined bishopric, his real reason being that, not having seen in everything with his Society at home, they might prefer not to confirm the nomination.

In the midst of all the anxiety and constant patient work that the affairs of the mission required came a terrible blow—the death of his mother. On December 8th Mrs. Hill writes:—

"Last night the English mail came, and before it came I had a presentiment of sorrow. Poor old Sid! you would have pitied him if you had seen him read the first lines. I can hardly realise that our mother is gone. She was a most true friend, and always acted like a mother to me, and I loved her very, very dearly. She was the most self-sacrificing woman I have ever known, and I never knew her to do a mean thing or speak an unkind word of any one: in fact, to me her character was almost unique in its Christ-likeness. . . . Sidney says it has taken an inspiration out of his life, and I am sure it is true. No one rejoiced more than that devoted mother when her 'boy' was encouraged in his work. But for her it is far better, and it is another link to the 'Home over there.'"

Mr. Bennet, who had been holding the fort in Onitsha, was now with them. He was on his way home on furlough, but finding of how much use he might be to the Bishop through his knowledge of Ibo, and for other reasons, he, with a true missionary spirit, resolved to turn back with them, and defer his holiday.

"S.S. 'ROQUETTE,' IN THE LAGOS ROADS,
"*Christmas Eve*, 1892.

"MY DEAREST M.,—

"I sent you a hurried note on Wednesday, for we were so pressed with all the copying and typewriting Sidney gave us to do. For the past week he kept the whole six of us employed till late in the evening, so that our English letters got rather neglected. The chief part of his work is done now, ending up with the Archbishop's report, and the travelling on the river itself begins. This is quite a typical part of it: we were rushed off from Lagos in a tremendous hurry, having at the last moment to get ready in half an hour or less; crossed the bar to the big steamer—a process which completely upset poor E.—and here we are still, and here we are likely to be till Monday! four days at anchor on board ship before we start away, and when we do start they take ten days going a distance they could do easily in twenty-four hours' steady steam! I need hardly say it is trying to one's patience; but all the mission people say that Africa seems to have been invented to teach one patience. However, we were all so weary with the work and heat of the past week that we do not much mind the delay here. Rest is so sweet. We are only just outside Lagos Bay, and can see the beach houses quite clearly. It would be well if we could fly over to spend Christmas Day at the ram-shackle old hut of the C.M.S., but E. says nothing will tempt her to cross the bar again. There was a great deal of sickness in Lagos when we left, and there had been several deaths. . . ."

At last they were on the way again for Onitsha, the goal of the journey for some of them. It is a station that has been occupied many years, and has had a flow and ebb in its spiritual life like many other places in Africa; but the great mass of its heathenism seems yet unreached.

On the way they stopped at Warri, a name almost unknown in England, yet boasting a British Consul. This gentleman kindly entertained the missionaries, and told them that he had walked for *four hours* from the Consulate inland, and it was one long street of dense population. He begged for some one to be sent to those tens of thousands. His last words to them were, "Well, Bishop, I hope you will do something for us before long; you really ought." Then they wandered into the bush, gathering exquisite flowers, and lost themselves, arriving at a strange village, where when the people caught sight of a white woman they raised a whoop, and they were soon surrounded by a great crowd, all pleasant and friendly. The Bishop was deeply moved; like his Master "he had compassion on the multitudes, because they were as sheep having no shepherd." And he resolved to make a great effort to send a teacher to a place so ready and so needing.

White women were a great novelty in these parts, for all the steamers do not call in at the creeks. In one little port there was a ludicrous scene: the natives came in shoals alongside to look at Mrs. Hill and her two companions. One of them went to the side of the ship without thinking, and shortly afterwards Mrs. Hill; the natives thought it must be the same person, and could not be made to believe that there were two, till the chief steward asked them to stand side by side, when the excitement became intense.

And thus the last days of the old year glided away on African waters, and the new found them on the river being conveyed in the Royal Niger Company's steamer *Boussa* to Onitsha, where they arrived on January 7th. The Christian population came out to meet them at the river side, and accompanied them to the mission houses, to which they walked, though it was the middle of the day and more than a mile's distance. The people sang the old hymn—

> "Through the love of God our Saviour
> All, all is well."

Among other queer things at Onitsha is the current coin, which is tobacco. It was startling at first to find a keg of it at the Mission House, but it soon proved not to be for the consumption of the missionaries, but for purposes of barter!

They arrived in the unhealthy season; one of the Roman Catholic Sisters died the day after, and then a man in the C.M.S. compound was taken ill. Mr. Proctor, who had taken Mr. Bennet's place and had consequently been alone the last few weeks, had had fever badly, but he spoke highly of the kindness and attention of the natives and the neighbourliness of the Roman Catholic priest, who had been three times to see him. They were now a party of seven, a larger contingent than the Society had ever been able to place there before in the history of the mission.

Very soon the chiefs began to "call." On such an occasion an important ceremony had to be gone through, the dividing of the Kola nut. The host or hostess brings it out on a plate, and the chief cracks it and chews a piece, after which all present take their share. The women were so delighted to see the white faces that they kissed one another in token of joy! The natives soon began to crowd in for medicine; they would sit about the verandah and watch everything, so that privacy and much writing were impossible.

The Bishop went to Asaba, as it was under consideration to remove the headquarters of the mission there, and he wished to see some land there. Mrs. Hill accompanied him, and they had the joy of finding twenty-two adult candidates for baptism and eight children. The first man who came forward was a king!

Next we read of Mrs. Hill and Miss F—— going to see a convert who had just given birth to twins. She was in a small room like a Chinese opium-den, with a huge wood fire burning in the middle!

It is disappointing to find that the old cruel superstition about twins still lingers. It is thought to be such a terrible disgrace for a woman to bear twins that they are never allowed to live. If the mother keeps them they inevitably disappear. The missionaries here sometimes try to rear them, but not apparently with any great success. At one time the mother's life was not safe. Now they have only to bear scorn and unkindness, for superstitions die hard. Mrs. Hill paid for the support of these babies, threatening to withdraw her weekly allowance if either of them died.

No sooner had the Bishop gone to Lokoja than Mrs. Hill had two of the party on her hands with fever. It was a very anxious time, but long practice had given her the habit of "casting her care," and she was carried through, not only in patience, but cheerfulness. Yet it must have been a terrible strain, for she could not get at her husband; and the ladies' little house being in another part of the compound, she was kept continually going from one house to the other day and night. And to cross an African compound by night is no pleasant trip. It means very careful picking the way and holding up the skirts to avoid the swarms of ants that you do not want to attach to your person or to bring into your house.

Food is always more or less of a difficulty in these regions. Bread and water is a proverbial expression for privation; but what if we could get neither bread nor water? All the water at Onitsha had to be brought a mile by bearers, so they had to be economical, and could not afford themselves baths, which are almost a necessity in the tropics, though they found Turkish baths a good substitute. And as for bread, Mrs. Hill says pathetically: "For three or four days I have not seen bread of *any* kind, and it is so difficult to eat bacon with very hard cabin biscuits!" But little do true-hearted missionaries reck of such things.

The Bishop's occupations at Onitsha were multifarious—from surveying in the woods to cooking in the kitchen. For some time he was head cook, and the lady missionaries worked under him. The heathen all loved him, for he had always a kind word for them, and was ready to do anything for them. Once an old heathen chief sent him his huge variegated umbrella to mend, and the Bishop spent a whole evening mastering the job, and returned it whole, much to the delight of its owner. They called him their father, and mourned him long and sincerely.

Before leaving Onitsha the Bishop invited the native pastors or schoolmasters from different ports to meet for three days' services ; and, as they could not be accommodated in the mission compound, he paid the expenses both of them and their wives. It was a most refreshing time to the missionaries, for it was the only time they had the comfort of hearing the services in English.

In February the Bishop and Mrs. Hill started on the return journey. They stayed at Akassa, New Calabar, Brass, and Bonny on the way, and the Bishop had much to try him, yet in speaking of that time afterwards he was able to tell of wonderful answers to prayer, and upholding grace under difficult circumstances.

As for the voyage, the heat was almost unbearable, for the *Boussa* stuck on a sandbank the first Sunday, and of course it is much more difficult to endure the sun when the vessel is not moving. Here Mrs. Hill found a little bit of ministry to keep her going. There were a Roman Catholic priest and a Sister on board, and the latter was taken with fever. They had no medicine, and no wraps of any sort, and the poor woman would have fared badly had she not fallen into such kindly hands. It appears that great numbers of Roman Catholics die on African stations, for so little is done for their comfort.

At Lagos the Bishop met Rev. H. H. Dobinson and Rev. Melville Jones, with whom he was glad to confer before returning home, and then they gladly set their faces towards England, though the joy was chastened by the thought of the loving mother who was no longer there to welcome them.

Some visible fruit of the Bishop's visit was shown in his being accompanied home by two earnest and devoted native clergymen, whom he had selected to present to the Archbishop as suitable for the office of Assistant-Bishops.

The Rev. Isaac Oluwole was the child of Christian parents at Abeokuta. He was educated there and at Lagos, and afterwards at Fourah Bay College, Sierra Leone, where he was among the first three who graduated in connection with Durham University. He has filled many posts in C.M.S. work, and was Master of the grammar school at Lagos, at the same time ministering at St. Peter's Church, where he won the respect and confidence of Bishop Hill.

The Rev. Charles Phillips has a more romantic history, for his father was one of the rescued slaves brought to Freetown by a British man-of-war. He also has been engaged both in pastoral and educational work, and both have been for several years in priest's orders, and are men of experience and devotion.

CHAPTER IX

CONSECRATION, AND DEPUTATION WORK

"Be to the flock of Christ
a shepherd, not a wolf;
feed them, devour them not.
Hold up the weak,
heal the sick,
bind up the broken,
bring again the outcasts,
seek the lost.
Be so merciful
that you be not too remiss;
so minister discipline
that you forget not mercy."

From the "Consecration of Bishops,"
Book of Common Prayer.

CHAPTER IX

CONSECRATION, AND DEPUTATION WORK

LITTLE remains to be told, for the few events, important though they were, between the return home and the final departure, stand out from a background of incessant, and, in some aspects, monotonous work. There was the visit to Durham, when the three Bishops received their Doctor's degree and enjoyed intercourse with Bishop Westcott, of whose writings Bishop Hill had the profoundest admiration, and whom he rejoiced to have the privilege of knowing.

The mere list of places visited on deputation nearly takes away one's breath. He held meetings and preached sermons in forty-four cities and large towns, beside a great many in London and the neighbourhood. Though intensely longing to see more of his children, whom he was so soon to leave behind, he never refused an invitation where it was possible to accept it, looking upon every opportunity to make known the needs of Africa as a sacred trust for which he was responsible; and well, indeed, did he fulfil it!

On St. Peter's Day the consecration took place of

the three Bishops for Africa and the new Bishop of Norwich. No one who was present in the grand Cathedral of our Metropolis will ever forget the dignity and solemnity of that service. There are times when the reality of the union in the one Body forces itself in a special manner upon us, and this was one of them. The sight of the two earnest and devout brethren from Western Africa, so soon to be admitted to the highest Order in the Church, helped one to realise how all barriers of race and colour break down in Him in whom "there is neither Jew nor Greek, circumcision nor uncircumcision, barbarian, Scythian, bond nor free." The Chancel, densely packed with reverent worshippers, re-echoed to the strains of loveliest music exalting Him who on His cross and from His throne has drawn and is drawing souls unto Himself from every nation under heaven. The beautiful pathetic voice of the Archbishop of Canterbury was in itself music. Then there was the impressive sermon by the Bishop of St. Andrews on the words, "Jesus Christ, the same yesterday, to-day, and for ever." It was remarkable not only for the force of its language and the beauty of its thoughts, but for the counsels so lovingly given and so specially applicable to the need of the African Bishops. When he spoke of never receiving their clergy without a prayer, nor sending them away without a blessing, one felt how that one counsel, honestly carried out, would spiritualise the relation between the Bishops and the pastors under them.

"God only knows," he said in conclusion, and the words have a ring of prophecy about them now, "how you shall be led into the deep valley of Gethsemane, into the darkness of Calvary; God only knows when and how in your lonely chamber—over-tired, over-wrought, in this busy, hurrying age—Satan shall darken every experience of your life and no voice rise but this, 'My God, my God, why hast Thou forsaken me?' God knows, my brethren, but Jesus Christ is the same yesterday, to-day, and for ever, whatever that 'for ever' may import. Only be still, be quiet; never, never forget to have a quiet hour; never, if matters have taken it from you in the week, fail to have a quiet day. Believe Christ will govern the Church better than you can govern it, and that your way of furthering the kingdom of Christ is to let Him take you, as He takes you to-day, to be a star in His right hand, to be guided by His eye; and that that can only be when you are alone with Him, and you commune with your own heart, and are still. God will keep you and make you more than conquerors in the power of that Christ who is the same yesterday, to-day, and for ever."

A very large number gathered at the Holy Table, where the new Bishops assisted the Bishops of Oxford and St. Albans.

After his consecration, engagements crowded thick and fast into the few weeks that Bishop Hill would fain have given to children and friends. But duty came ever first with him. It is easy to be wise after the event; one wonders whether it would have been possible to hold him back, whether that sad verdict might have been averted, repeated so often by one and another who was with him at the last, "Bishop Hill came out thoroughly over-worked."

Has not the Christian Church something yet to learn about the care and preservation of bodily health and strength?

There was much to interest and comfort the Bishop's large warm heart in the visits he paid, often hurriedly, on deputation work. Writing of his visit to B., near a large sea-port, the clergyman's wife who entertained him says:—

"His visit was a time of blessing to all in the house. He was so bright, and seemed so very near the Master. I so well remember when, after a tiring day, and having addressed two crowded meetings, he gathered us for family prayer. That prayer was one never to be forgotten. He seemed to forget no one, and no country or class. When saying good-bye to our coachman he shook his hand heartily and said, 'If we don't meet again here we shall in the glory.' The coachman said he never felt any one's death so much, and we find so many in the village felt as though a near relative had gone, so closely did he twine himself round all our hearts. My little boys always prayed for him daily, and were so fond of him."

It was very sweet to the Bishop to know of these children's prayer; he more than once alluded to it with pleasure.

Much was written at the time of the Bishop's clearly defined policy for West African Missions, so for the benefit of those who did not enter into the question it may be as well to give a few outlines of his hopes for the future of the Church there. He was very profoundly impressed with the claims of the natives and the duty of doing justice to them. He thought it unfair and ill-judged to compare them with English congregations, a very common fault arising from the tendency to ignore history. As he argued, they are to be judged by what they *are*, contrasted with what they *were*. And when one thinks of the centuries of enlightenment we in England have had, it is rather for us to hide our faces in the dust, than to disparage the moral attainments of a race that was in some parts cannibal yesterday.

He did not think that conformity to native ways in dress and in food was desirable. The native dress in the Soudan he regarded as connected with Mohammedan religion—indeed identified with it. As for the native food, it was all very well, if not cooked in native fashion.

Geographically his plan was to attack the Soudan from two points—Yoruba and the Niger. Beyond Abeokuta is a large native town called Oyo. This is our most northern station, and the Bishop wanted to make it a centre. He had already in his mind a well-known native clergyman whom he hoped to send there. Nowadays it is no surprise to hear of a town of 300,000 inhabitants right in the middle of Africa; such is Illorin, and the Bishop longed to take it in the name of the Lord, and let the Gospel be its first introduction to European civilisation, there being no trade there yet. Will it be done? It needs men and money.

From the Niger side Lokoja would still be the centre for the Hausa country.

It was very near the Bishop's heart to have a training home at Onitsha under his own direction for native agents and their wives, and also to build there a hospital as the centre of medical mission work. And then he was very anxious for a steamer, for he very reasonably thought that the mistakes made in relation to the *Henry Venn* might be avoided, or what is the meaning of learning by experience? It could be built at a much less expense, and the cost of keeping it up would be little more than is paid to the Royal Niger Company for the accommodation in their steamers.

The Bishop spoke of these things constantly at the last before leaving England. He hoped that money would flow in and men be called out as soon as the real wants of this corner of the Dark Continent were made known. He talked and prayed and thought and preached Africa, and Africa only.

A friend has supplied us with the following interesting account of the Bishop as "Deputation," which comes in appropriately here:—

"How many links of sacred friendship supporters of the C.M.S. can date from the first visits of those who have come beneath their roof, representing this great Church Society for the evangelisation of the world! With what anxious feelings we have often awaited the arrival of an unknown 'deputation'!

We have wondered whether he would inspire and strengthen our weak faith; whether God's fire would characterise his missionary utterances, thus setting our hearts aglow for the needs of a perishing world. Many, very many, 'deputations' have come and gone, leaving with us holier aspirations and quickened zeal. None more truly than the Rev. J. S. Hill, who first visited us as a C.M.S. 'deputation' on May 16th, 1892. He arrived unexpectedly in the early morning, and was by mistake shown into a room where I was busily preparing for a Parish Sale. His bright, genial greeting made me at home with him at once, and instinctively I experienced that feeling of trust which ever comes to us in the presence of the good and true. His ready helpfulness soon manifested itself, and in a short time he was carrying the heavy boxes of work downstairs, ready as he always was to help one just in the way most needed at the time. If only 'deputations' knew the joy and gladness they carry with them when they bring God's sunshine in their hearts and faces as Mr. Hill did, those who receive them would more often find that they 'have entertained angels unawares.' Everywhere he won hearts in his deputation work by his hearty, loving manner. My first impression of his character was his breadth of sympathy, an impression that deepened as our friendship grew. He was very forbearing in his judgments of others, and tolerant to those who viewed things from different standpoints. How singularly he made the joys and sorrows of his friends his own! He ever spake the truth and nothing but the truth to them, but it was so mingled with love that it always helped and strengthened them to remedy that which was lacking in their character or experience. He helped to dispel their doubts and clear away their mists of difficulty where others would perhaps only have rebuked the doubt.

"We soon found out that Africa's great needs lay very near his heart. How he rejoiced at the prospect of going there again, where, as he said, the greatest triumphs of the devil had taken place, and where, he believed, would be the greatest triumphs of the Cross! He was praying earnestly at that time that the C.M.S. might be guided in the choice of a Bishop for West Africa. How very far from his own thoughts it was that he himself would be called to this high and holy office!

"After a few short weeks he was with us again for our C.M.S. anniversary. His sermons and addresses were alike characterised by freshness and vigour of thought rarely met with in these days of stereotyped phrases and conventional modes of expression. He spoke to the hearts of his audience, never once over their heads. In the evening meeting his own heart seemed overflowing with the needs of the world, and he said he felt as Dr. Moffat did, when speaking at a large meeting, when he could only say again and again: '*It's a glorious work, it's a glorious work—co-workers with God!*' He described most graphically the incident when he was saved from drowning during his first visit to Africa. As he was floating on the water he thought of those praying at home, and it strengthened him. Years after he heard from that devoted servant of Christ, the late Major Malan, that at a certain hour every day he had borne him up in prayer. Mr. Hill said he could not help wondering if Major Malan's prayer had not been a link in the chain of his preservation. His closing words were intensely earnest: 'Beloved friends, I am going out to Africa again because there are 20,000,000 in the Soudan who have never heard the Gospel. Most thankful shall I be for your prayers. *Pray for me.*' From that time numberless prayers went up for him in this parish. (On his last visit in September 1893 I overheard a working man say, as he wrung his hand, in parting, 'Good-bye, sir; you've left a prayer-book in our hearts!')

In August of the same year he came to us at Bournemouth, where we were staying, and gave a missionary address at St. John's, Boscombe. It was an intensely solemn appeal for Africa's crying needs. In this address he told how when a young man he visited the Rev. J. N. Darby (who, whatever his mistakes, was a most saintly man). He was lying on a sick-bed not expecting to recover, and he said to him words which made a deep impression: 'Young man, *live* in the heavenlies. *Begin* there; I am *ending* there.'

"Again it was our privilege to welcome him at

our annual C.M.S. gathering in June 1893, and we saw the needs of Africa were burnt more deeply still into his heart. At our preparatory missionary prayer meeting he spoke stirring words on obedience the test of discipleship. On Sunday he pleaded with burning earnestness for the millions of souls soon to be committed to his charge, as he was now appointed Bishop in Western Equatorial Africa. 'The activities of God's love for the world cannot be quenched, but are we rising to our privilege as co-workers with Him for the salvation of souls?'

"Once again he visited us, in September, spending ten days under our roof. Every member of our family and household loved him, and he soon won the hearts of all our parishioners.

"He had since his last visit been consecrated to the high and holy office of a Bishop in the Church of God, but he was clothed more than ever with humility, ready at all times and in all ways to be the 'servant of all.' This visit brought salvation to the one unconverted member of our household.

"At this time our Annual Conference for the deepening of the spiritual life was being held. He preached the Conference sermon; it was felt to be one of the most powerful and comprehensive he had ever preached. The subject was John iii. 34. The last words on his private notes for this sermon are: '*Broken-heartedness. Been up all night.*' Surely *this* was the secret of its striking power. May God give us such compassion for the sins of the world!

From Photograph by Clarke, Bury St. Edmunds.]

Yours loving brother in Him
J. S. Hill.

"Throughout the Conference God used him mightily. To Church people and Nonconformists alike his message was 'in demonstration of the Spirit and of power.'

"On the last Sunday morning a large number of working men belonging to various denominations attended the service in our church to hear him—a witness truly to his catholicity of spirit, which drew people of all shades of thought around him. The next time this same body of men attended the service, it was as a token of respect to his memory, on that first Sunday after the Epiphany when the sad news reached us from the West Coast of his home-call.

"Through these last days of fellowship he was more than ever a sweet savour of Christ. He was ever ready to do a kindly act for any one. The day-school teachers were anxious to attend the Conference missionary meeting; the Bishop heard this, and went himself to ask if the time might be given them. His addresses during the Conference were singularly helpful, specially one on 'Cleansing.' How many incidents live in our hearts of kindly deeds prompted by his loving thoughtfulness! He was very anxious that a clergyman whom he loved should attend the Keswick Convention. We heard after his death that he said to a mutual friend: 'How can we manage it? Do you think it would be easier for him if I stayed away from the Convention and took his duty?'

"Many testimonies could be given from this parish

and neighbourhood of the manifold way in which Bishop Hill was used to old and young, to rich and poor alike. He felt strongly and impressed on others the sacred nature of opportunity. I can never forget his faithful word to one who felt she had lost an opportunity of witnessing for Christ. In his outspoken way he said: 'That opportunity will never come to you. An opportunity given and lost is never, never given back again.' Whenever he visited us he talked, as was his wont, for hours at night. Latterly he pleaded with impassioned earnestness the claims of those who have never heard the Gospel. . . . He besought with tears that the tent pegs might be loosened and the stakes set less firmly in the ground. One present then heard through this faithful ambassador of the Cross his own call 'to launch out yet further into the deep and let down his net for a draught' in the regions beyond. He knew well that going to Africa meant the possibility of a life laid down. Yet for that land he was as ready to die as live, should the Lord so call. Even before going out in 1892 he said to me of himself and dear Mrs. Hill: 'We are both going to a deadly climate; one or both of us may fall.' I said I could not bear to think of such a possibility. With a bright smile, though tears were in his eyes, he said cheerfully, 'That's all right,' and soon his merry ringing laugh was heard again.

"On All Saints' Day, after the Gleaners' Anniversary, we bade farewell to the Bishop and Mrs. Hill, 'until the day break and the shadows flee away.' During that meeting Mrs. Hill gave me her last message, 'He that loseth His life for My sake shall find it.' I thank God I had the privilege of her friendship as well as the Bishop's. She was one of the most sensible, unselfish women I have ever met. Very practical, yet withal so loving and humble, she, like the Bishop, had wonderful powers of sympathy, and so ably undertook his correspondence.

"The following letter she wrote to me on Mrs. Douglas Hooper's death, at Jilore, seems strangely appropriate now, and has an added meaning of comfort and strength :—

"'I feel afraid of writing to you, for human sympathy does seem so feeble in the presence of a great sorrow like yours; and sometimes it almost seems like an intrusion into one's innermost being that feels harsh and unwelcome. But I can only assure you that I *do* pray that the "God of *all* comfort" may speak to your heart in such a way that you may very soon be able to praise Him that the dear one is in His bright presence, and that from lacking this "nether spring" you have drunk much deeper from the "upper spring." A big sorrow, I think, always does this for the children of the King. Of course to *our* vision it seems sometimes as if those most needed were taken away; but our Father makes no mistakes, and this home-call of Edith Douglas Hooper certainly means for her joy, of which we can have no conception till we too are in the immediate presence of the King; while for her friends left behind, I believe it will be just the Good Shepherd leading them through the narrow lonely path that He may bring them out into a wealthy place.

"'Oh! dear ——, He has done it, and you can trust *Him*.

"'"Praise God the Shepherd is so sweet!
Praise God the country is so fair!
We could not hold them from His feet,
We can but haste to meet them there!"

"'With heartfelt love and sympathy,

"'Ever yours in Him,

"'LUCY HILL.'"

This letter, which fitly closes Mrs. ——'s account, is a beautiful pendant to the one Mrs. Hill wrote on her marriage, in which she expressed her willingness to die, if God so willed it, for Africa. From first to last she was thoroughly sincere and consistent in her devotion, and the pain of loss to those who loved them both so well is often alleviated by the thought of the "readiness to be offered" which characterised husband and wife alike.

Well do we recall those sunny September days at S——, enjoying a fulness of intercourse with our beloved friend which could not in the course of our busy lives be often attained. One day he rowed a few friends on the beautiful river, and Mr. and Mrs. Binns, of East Africa, were of the party. It was one of those days that stand out in golden light amid the thickly gathering shadows of life. The calm full river, the lovely landscape crowned with the Cathedral spire, the happy chastened talk of those men who were going to travel soon on rivers and through country haunted by fever and befouled with sin and idolatry,—yet how little we realised "it is the last time!"

On the last Sunday the Bishop preached in the afternoon in the Cathedral* to a vast crowd. It was another fervid appeal to come and die for Africa. Most of the party then gathered together at F—— Rectory came up to London a few days after to be present at the dismissal meetings. We gathered together at St. Bride's round the Holy Table. Friends from all parts had made an effort to be present that day. No one who heard the Bishop's sermon on "The Fellowship of His Sufferings" will ever forget it. No notes, however full, can give any adequate idea of the power he had of swaying an audience. It was the intense reality, the baring of his heart, the force of his convictions, which made men listen almost in awe as he poured out his message. There was a young man there that day who was in the midst of as successful a career as heart could desire. He had taken two scholarships, and passed brilliantly into Oxford. He was being spoken of as likely to make a mark in the literary world in the near future. Of godly parentage and personally religious, life was yet very attractive; but as Bishop Hill lifted up the Cross of shame, and the light from heaven fell on the self-sacrificing King of Glory, he began to see something of the beauty of following the Lord fully,

* Salisbury.

of laying all his gifts and powers at the pierced feet. "He was not disobedient to the heavenly vision." He is now going forth as a missionary to India.

This is only one special instance of the effect of his burning words. Though he sometimes expressed himself disappointed that he had not obtained all the men whom he had pleaded for, seed was sown which perhaps will bear fruit in a later generation; and to how many his sermons were an inspiration for the self-sacrifice of daily life!

A lady who had gone to the Keswick Convention on one occasion, very heavily laden, remarked with tears of gratitude:—

"My message came on the last Sunday. I was walking sadly home to my lodgings in the evening; my way lay past the big tent. I heard a voice I did not know, and I waited a moment to listen. I shall never forget it, I was riveted to the spot. The love of God seemed to come to me in a new light as that yearning passionate voice poured out its eager pleadings with sinners 'to look unto Him and be saved.' I did not know till afterwards that the preacher was Bishop Hill."

On All Saints' Day Bishop Hill, as Gleaners' "Own Missionary," presided at the Gleaners' Union Meeting in Exeter Hall, to which allusion has already been made. He gave some interesting facts of the response that had been made to the needs of the Niger Mission. When he went down to Exeter, a clergyman who had intended to give £250 to build a Mission Church, after hearing the Bishop offered to double the amount. It happened that Bishop Hill had just had a letter from Mr. Dobinson asking him if he could raise £500 for a new church at Onitsha. Thus he had the exact sum. Mrs. Bishop's (Isabella Bird's) wonderfully touching address, which she rose from a sick-bed to give, has been so extensively circulated that we need only allude to it here. It made a profound impression. None in that vast gathering will surely ever forget the parting words of the Chairman compressed into the last three minutes. He said :—

"I have three words to leave with you, an *inspiration*, a *fellowship*, a *sacrifice*. I knew one most powerful preacher, one who had been much used of God in the salvation of souls, and whenever you heard that man preach you would often discover that just as he looked down at what you would think to be notes, he seemed to get some fresh inspiration. And if you were to go and look at those notes you would see just one word, JESUS. I want you, beloved Gleaners, to get a fresh *inspiration* to-night from that loving one, Jesus. Look upon Him that you may get a fresh inspiration for this year's service. And then, a *fellowship*. I do not know if you have ever read the remarkable passage in the Life of Henry Martyn, in which he gives an account of how he spent a night in agonising sorrow, which was the result of a thought coming to his mind of the value of a soul to God. He began to think of the various outcasts in India as being quite as dear to God as the kings of Britain. And that night he spent in prayer, in tears, in sorrow over souls. Beloved Gleaners, I pray God that this year you may know something of the fellowship with the

Lord Jesus Christ in His sorrow for souls. And now that other word, *sacrifice*. A noble youth of Rome, who discovered the riches of God's grace in Christ, and became a follower of the Lord, went to Hermas with a desire. 'What,' said he, 'can I do in return for such love as this?' Hermas took out the noble young fellow and showed him something of the sin of Rome, and as he pointed out here and there something of the need of its souls, he said: 'Here you will find an altar, and there become the sacrifice.' Look upon the fields, white unto the harvest. Look upon the millions that are without Christ in the world to-night in their awful sin, and you will find an altar, and may God help you, beloved Gleaners, to be a sacrifice."

Thus he went forth to sacrifice, but what a glad sacrifice it was! Amid all the desperately hard work of those last weeks he maintained his boyish spirits. He perfectly exemplified the paradox, "Sorrowful yet always rejoicing." A highly characteristic incident comes from the Archbishop. When he and his two native colleagues were leaving Addington, and good-byes had been said, Bishop Hill turned round and said: "There's only one thing I regret; I've got the men I wanted, and I've got the money I wanted, but I did want to snowball these two fellows!"

CHAPTER X

SAFE HOME IN PORT

"And oh! if any think this story sad,
The pity is for them, who yet must learn
What Life is,—and what Death; and to those souls
Who read both only in the pure, white light
Where God abides and teaches, those who fix
Their eager gaze upon the things not seen,
I whisper, 'See, this picture is not Death,
But risen Life, another hero-face
Stamp'd with high victory before he fell
Triumphant where he fail'd, crown'd on his Cross,
And like his Lord, self-sentenced to his doom.'"

ELEANOR FURSKE

CHAPTER X

SAFE HOME IN PORT

AT last the final start was made. On November 21st, 1893, the large party of missionaries met at Liverpool and embarked next day on board the *Batanga.* The morning was so stormy that there was a doubt whether she could start, and although she got out, the pilot was carried in to Milford Haven, it being impossible to land him at the usual place. Better weather soon prevailed, and as the passengers and missionaries ventured on deck next day, the kind helpfulness of Bishop and Mrs. Hill began to be, as it ever was, conspicuous, giving up their chairs, choosing the least comfortable quarters, making friends with every one. "Their tenderness and watchfulness never flagged," writes one who was present, "and not one of the large missionary party was left out in the cold."

Then began a time of spiritual teaching and valuable technical instruction, on which the survivors look back with lively gratitude. Every day the missionary party met in some quiet part of the deck where they would not disturb others, and the Bishop conducted a Bible reading with them, taking chiefly the First Epistle to the Corinthians, which he looked upon as the missionary's vade-mecum, both on questions of personal holiness and those which arise from contact with the heathen. All were encouraged to ask questions, and when the allotted hour was over the Bishop was generally to be seen leaning over the bulwarks in earnest talk with one or other of the young clergy, discussing some point that had arisen during the reading. How they valued a quiet talk with him, conscious that when the busy missionary life in Africa had once begun such opportunities would rarely occur!

The Sunday services were unique, inasmuch as the congregation was ministered to by two Bishops, one of them a native (Bishop Phillips had gone on before). The passengers, ship's officers, and crew were all eager in their attendance. In the morning the Holy Communion was administered. There was a Bible reading at three, and in the evening an important service was held for the sailors in their own quarters, to which many others found their way and listened unobserved. The monotony of the voyage was first broken by a visit to Grand Canary, where the missionaries spent a long day. The Bishop was the merriest of the party, but it was observed that in the evening he seemed much exhausted. From thence the telegram was sent to the C.M.S. at home, announcing all well, which filled so many hearts in England with thankfulness and joy.

We extract from one of the Bishop's rare letters, posted here to his children :—

" . . . We very, very often are talking of you both, and if your little ears burn you may be sure old Dad is talking of you. It has been a very great help and comfort to us to feel you are so brave and good about it all. You may be quite certain of this, that the loving Lord and Saviour will make up to you in His love, and His care, and His blessing, all the loving sacrifice you make for Him. Is it not lovely to think of our having such a nice passage, the wind fair all the way, and so calm, when it has been so rough before, and so many have suffered? It is quite like summer-time—so warm, so bright—and we are just going to land for an hour or so. Mother was saying this morning it would be such a nice trip for you to come and meet us with darling old Auntie—you, I am sure, would enjoy it to-day—and we could, perhaps, manage to have a month together here before the many meetings, which take away father so much from home. My darlings, I want you to be very, very dear loving treasures to Auntie. I want you to keep very near to the side of Jesus all the time. Just have the joy of pleasing Him in everything, and don't think you need wait until you are older, but begin now to so try and serve the Lord that you may have many, very many jewels in your crown by-and-by. Pray for dear mother and father, and remember the Lord Jesus has always answered your prayers. And don't forget that to *be* what the Lord Jesus wants you to be is even better than serving Him. Now, darlings, the Lord be with you and keep you, both in body and soul, and make your peace and joy to be in Himself more and more. With our very, very warmest love,

"Your own loving
"DAD."

The next letter has a special interest, inasmuch as it was the last ever penned to his children. After his arrival at Lagos, Mrs. Hill says, "Sidney is *entirely* occupied in African affairs" :—

"S.S. 'BATANGA,' *December 5th*, 1893.

"MY OWN DARLING PETS,—

"I have been thinking that it will be very near Christmas by the time this gets home; so I must first wish you both a very, very happy Christmas. When I was a boy I don't think I liked Christmas as much as I do now, because it means so much more to me. I used to like Good Friday and Easter, because it told me of His death and His love for me; but now I sometimes think it was His birth as Man made Him known to us as we know Him now. I hope you will see what a wonderful gift He is. God's Christmas gift is Jesus.

"You know since I have been on board it has been my birthday, and the Captain had quite a nice tea arranged for me. Was it not kind? Everybody on board has been so very good to us, so friendly, and we have been so happy together in our work and in our prospects of work. I often wish you could be with us. I have seen some fish this time we have never seen before. . . . Though it is very hot to-night, yet I don't think I feel it so much as some of them. . . . Mother is doing Mr. Wigram's letter (typing)—a long one I have written upon the training of agents for the mission field. I wonder when you both will be ready for training, and able to come out with us. Mother is so much better, I think, and I do hope she will keep well all the time. Now, my precious pets, I do hope all is going on well with you. I suppose we shall not hear a word from you for another month, so until then we shall not know how any of you are. May the loving Lord keep you both and dearest Auntie in His holy keeping! Keep yourselves in His love. Remember how much more He can do for you than any one else, and how very, very near He is to you, and try—oh! do, my precious darlings, try—to please Him in everything. With our very, very best love to you and Auntie,

"Your ever-loving old

"DAD."

On December 6th they reached Sierra Leone, and on landing went straight to Canon Taylor Smith's house, where they found that a missionary meeting had been arranged in the Wilberforce Memorial Hall to welcome them. As soon as the *Batanga's* gun fired, the bellman was sent round to gather the people together, and the hall was soon crammed with people, scarcely a white face to be seen among them.

All the missionaries were on the platform, opposite which they read, in large letters, "The Church of Sierra Leone greets you." It was an inspiring sight, and it must have been well calculated to cheer the hearts of those who had left all to carry the name of Christ to the Dark Continent to hear those five hundred voices joining in the grand old hymns "Jesus shall reign" and "All hail the power of Jesu's name."

At Sierra Leone two of the party were left—Mr. Alvarez to help in work at Fourah Bay College, and Miss Thornewell. The rest soon went on board again, taking back with them Bishop Phillips and Mr. Tugwell, who had preceded them to Sierra Leone. To this Bishop Hill had looked forward with great delight, saying when a little anxious on one occasion, "It will be all right when Tugwell comes."

Everything was done by the missionaries to give pleasure to their fellow-passengers, and they took care to partake without grudging in their innocent amusements. They joined in two concerts, and twice the Bishop illustrated a story with his magic lantern. At the last of these entertainments there was very hearty cheering and expressions of thanks to the one whom all felt had contributed so much to the comfort and pleasure of the voyage.

And so the last Sunday came round. Bishop Oluwole preached by special request in the morning, and in the evening Bishop Hill gave his parting word. Miss Maxwell says:—

"I don't remember the text, but can never forget his glowing words as he told of the preciousness of his Lord and besought each one to know Him and love Him, saying there was something in Him too wonderful and beautiful for words to describe—that if we only saw it no pleading would be needed, but that to know it we must appropriate Him."

From Photograph by T. C. Turner & Co., 10, Barnsbury Park, N.)

Yours affectionately
Lucas Hill

The following Tuesday they reached the bar outside Lagos. All were sorry to leave the *Batanga* and their kind Captain. As the good-byes were being said he remarked to Mrs. Hill, who was one of the last to leave, "Well, this is the most precious load that has ever landed at one time at Lagos."

The method of landing would not commend itself generally to ladies. They were lowered in barrels into a canoe, and again hoisted in the same way from the canoe to the steamer which was waiting to carry them in—a process which must have taken some time, one would think.

How wonderful that welcome must have seemed to those arriving in Africa for the first time! What high hopes, what fulfilled aspirations were theirs! In all ages no doubt missionaries have felt the same. As they stood up and sang "All hail the power of Jesu's name," an echo came to them over the dividing waters, and every moment they descried more clearly the figures on the beach, until they realised that they were only one part of a mighty congregation uniting together, black and white, in the exaltation of their common Lord.

But behind this outward unity there was a background of disaffection which soon made itself felt. The Assistant-Bishops did not receive the warm welcome which Bishop Hill had hoped for, and he was keenly disappointed to find questions re-opening which he thought he had left closed. It would be a grave mistake were we to enter now on these subjects of disagreement in these pages; yet it is impossible to represent truthfully the condition of mind and body which made the Bishop so ready a prey to fever, without alluding to the depressing influences which produced that condition. The man who perhaps knew best says that the cold reception and unfriendly attitude of some "preyed upon his sensitive mind and distressed and broke his loving heart." Such language may be, indeed, the hyperbole of affection, but there can be no doubt about the pain and disappointment he felt. Physically he was in a worn-out condition; he had been working incessantly in England up to the last minute, as we have seen, and he missed the potent stimulus of thorough sympathy and co-operation which he had joyfully anticipated.

There was, however, a ray of comfort in the cordial relations between himself and Bishop Ingham, with whom he had much business to transact. There is something touching in the following sentences, which occur in a letter from a home-going missionary whom he and Mrs. Hill accompanied across the bar. She was anxious about his health and told him so, and what she elicited in reply

"did not tend," she writes, "to allay my anxiety. I said what I could in remonstrance, and he told me he had just been to breakfast with Bishop Ingham, and spoke of *his* calm way of facing difficulties and of the sunshine he threw on them, and he added, 'He has been such a help and comfort to me.' He had gone to breakfast feeling very depressed, but Bishop's Ingham's fellowship and the prayer they had had together had done him so much good. And he concluded, 'And now I am as lively as a sand-boy.' I can hear his ringing laugh as he said it."

How characteristic is this little incident! No one was ever more susceptible to sympathy, as no one was more capable of giving it. One looks with pleasure on the picture of the two Bishops meeting in that spiritual wilderness, like David and Jonathan in the wood (meeting but to part for ever!), to strengthen one another's hands in God.

He was, of course, kept busy from the moment he landed. We pass from stormy meetings where he patiently strove to set things right that had gone wrong again, and notice with pleasure his first Confirmation on Christmas Eve, then the services on Christmas Day, on both of which occasions the Bishop preached.

Then came the last Sunday, when in the evening he preached a powerful sermon on the text, "Died Abner as a fool dieth," the subject being "three lives"—a wasted life, a disappointing life, a worthless life. And he pleaded earnestly with the young men present not to disappoint the Lord's expectations of them, but to begin with that new year to live such lives as might be worthy of Him. It was ever a favourite theme with him, the importance of the gift of life, the baseness and ingratitude of frittering it away or misusing it. We cannot believe that his last appeal was without fruit. And so the Old Year passed away and a New Year dawned which to six of the mission party was to have no ending, but to merge into the days of eternity.

Mrs. Hill's last letters are dated December 30th, with a postscript of January 1st. Full of loving counsel to her children about little matters of health, such things as occupy a mother's thoughts, they mention little inconveniences—a passing cloud of locusts which had left the country bare when they swept by, prickly heat in her eyes which made writing somewhat painful—but no hint of coming disaster, no foreshadowing of the silence never more to be broken "till Jesus comes."

In her letter to her sister almost the last words are the text of a sermon of Bishop Oluwole's before he started for Abeokuta, "To me to live is Christ." A week later we know she could finish the verse from blessed experience.

They all went to early service on that New Year's morning, and then the Bishop set off to visit a young Scotchman in the hospital who was dangerously ill. In the meantime there was a report that the steamer by which they hoped to go on to Onitsha was in the roads. It turned out that she was not able to take them, but in any case they could not have gone, for Mrs. Hill adds: "Almost at the same moment I found Sister's hands and feet were icy cold, and saw in a moment she was 'in' for fever." This was the beginning. Miss Maxwell (known to the mission party, as at Mildmay, as Sister Louisa) was the first attacked and the only one who recovered of the Niger party.

The Bishop then had his last interview with Dr. Oluwole, who was starting for an episcopal tour in the Yoruba district. The latter remarked that he looked tired and worried, but he entered fully, as was his wont, into the plans for the work, which included careful consideration of candidates for ordination.

In the evening of the same day the Bishop became ill, and soon afterwards his wife.

Sister Louisa was moved over to the Girls' Seminary to make room for the invalids, and then began the fight of Love with Death. "I do not fear because of the fever," said the Doctor, as he examined the Bishop, "but I think very seriously of the state of his heart."

Mr. and Mrs. Vernall were unremitting in their care of the patients. (Alas! *their* case was harder, for Death separated *them*.) The young clergy were in and out, full of solicitude and anxiety to be of help. And so the sad days of that fatal week passed by. The Bishop spoke little, but in delirium he pleaded earnestly with souls.

"Ask—that young man if—there is any reason why—he should not take Christ as his Saviour," he once exclaimed eagerly. The ruling passion, strong in death, asserted itself.

The last words exchanged between husband and wife were on Thursday night, when the Bishop said, "I am going Home." Mrs. Hill heard him, and at once replied, "Yes, *we* are going Home."

His sufferings were intense.

On Friday morning he tried to say, "Pray," and as Mr. Vernall knelt by his side and prayed briefly that he might realise the presence and peace and rest of Jesus, and that the Great Physician would lay His hand upon him, he tried with difficulty to clasp his hand, and to say, "Amen." Very soon the prayer was answered. The Great Physician laid so strong a hand upon him that he could not choose but follow Him right through the dark valley, and

> "Where beyond these voices there is Peace."

This was Friday afternoon. Mrs. Hill still lay unconscious. Mr. Tugwell, in the long and interesting account from which these details are taken, draws a beautiful picture, which we who mourn would retain in our memories :—

"As I write the light of my lamp falls through the open doorway upon the sleeping, restful form of the Bishop, robed in his rochet by the loving hands of Bishop Phillips. Since his death a beautiful smile has lit up his otherwise haggard features."

Mrs. Hill never knew her loss: her call came a little after midnight. They kept their Epiphany Feast together in the presence of the Lord.

When Mr. Tugwell opened the visitors' book a day or two after, to make a note of the date of their departure to be with Christ, he found the Bishop's text under his name had been Rom. viii. 38, 39, and Mrs. Hill had written in full: "*Whosoever will lose his life for My sake shall find it.*"

At 4 p.m. (Saturday, January 6th, 1894) they were carried into Christ Church, where the first part of the funeral service was read, Bishop Phillips, Rev. H. Tugwell (now Bishop), Archdeacon Johnson, and several clergy, both native and of the mission party, being present, and a vast congregation filled the church and surrounded the grave. They sang in church, "For all Thy saints who from their labours rest," and "How sweet the hour;" while at the graveside,

"Hush! blessed are the dead,
In Jesu's arms who rest,"

stilled the lamentations of the warm-hearted people, to whom the loss of the Bishop was so sudden and so strange.

"Jesus, Lord of Glory, as *we* breast the tide,
Whisper Thou the story of the other side;
Where the saints are casting crowns before Thy feet,
Safe for everlasting, in Thyself complete!"

Unfortunately, there could not be communication with Onitsha, as the wire to Akassa was broken. So the two who were waiting there, Mr. Dobinson and Mr. Wilson, with the lady workers, had nothing to break the force of the blow when, instead of six whom they were expecting, the Bishop at their head, the news came that only one of the party was on his way. The distress was very great in the compound and out of it. The chiefs were coming in constantly with their lamentations and expressions of sympathy, while the wailing in the neighbourhood was something terrible to hear. The poor natives could only realise that their friend and father was not coming back to them, and they were inconsolable.

The Bishop's boy, Samuel, expressed no doubt the feelings of many in the following touching letter, which we transcribe just as it stands, feeling that it will be interesting to all who love the African.

The date is, of course, a mistake.

"It was on February that we receive the sad, sad news, which tells us that our dear Bishop and his wife were dead at Lagos when coming to us here on the Niger. We have been looking out for them in a very happy way; but at last we failed. The same day that we receive the sad news is the day that we expect to see him in the mission station at Onitsha. But when we receive the very sad news, we faint. It is a very marvellous thing in our eyes, but *God knows the better way of doing His work.*" (So the poor negro boy and the aged New Zealand Archdeacon had come to the same conclusion. See Introduction.) "The Bishop, as far as I can judge, is a man who has much power in God's work, and when preaching he is very desirous to people to understand him. The one that I am speaking (of) is just for a month and half, which he stays at Onitsha, January and February 1893. He laboured night and day as I see, having no time to rest. The chiefs of our country are seen every day in the mission station, and he settles many palavers for them, and they calls him the peacemaker. I, the same boy which is saying all these things, was his boy when he first came. I am an African boy, Onitsha on the Niger boy; he is very kind to everybody, great and small. Any time he asks any one to do something, he begins with, Will you? Everybody on the Niger loves him. He has done a great deal of work here. When he is coming, everything is kept till the Bishop comes. I believe he wants to make the mission here a very good one; I have heard and read how he tried very hard in England to work for us. But now God has taken him to be with Him. This is the Lord's doing, it is marvellous in our eyes. His wife, too, is very loving and gentle; both were loving in their lives, and in their death they were not divided. I must end here. If I had been with him a long time, I would have said many things about his kindness. But one thing I know, he is full of kindness to everybody.

"SAMUEL C. OBUYANWULU."

This boy had written a most touching letter to the Bishop when he was in England, entreating him to send him where he would be able to learn more, "whether in England or elsewhere, that I may be taught how to labour in the Lord's plenteous harvest. Why I tell you so quick is because I want it to be easier for you when you come back again; so that when I grow up I will be able to work and live for our Lord Jesus Christ." His postscript is: "May God help you in all your works; may He bless you and lead you with His Holy Spirit. Amen."

We have said that only one man of the Niger party reached Onitsha. Messrs. Sealey and Matthias died on the way up. The latter was ordained by Bishop Hill in October at St. Paul's, Onslow Square. A tender regard existed between them, and he felt the Bishop's loss keenly, yet so truly did he recognise the will of God to be "good, and acceptable, and perfect" that he was able to sign the letter of mournful details which he wrote from Lagos, "*Yours joyfully in Him.*" The child of earnest Christian parents, he early consecrated a vigorous youth of rare promise to the highest service. He had worked for three or four years at St. Paul's, Onslow Square, and at Cambridge, while reading for his degree. The last Sunday before leaving England he had preached in the mission-room connected with St. Paul's from the words: "I am now ready to be offered, and the time of my departure is at hand"; and in an unfinished private letter written from Lagos he had written: "I want to be just willing to be anything as long as His name may be glorified in my body, whether by life or by death." He died in the Forcados river, and they carried his body some way up the country to the compound of a European who kindly offered this last resting-place that he might not lie surrounded by the heathen.

Well might the lonely brother missionary left

behind have expressed himself in Trench's beautiful words :—

> "Brief words we read of faith and prayer,
> Beside that hasty grave,
> Then turned away and left him there,
> The gentle and the brave.
>
> "And, comforted, I praised the grace
> Which him had led to be
> An early seeker of that Face
> Which he should early see."

Mr. Sealey died a little later on, and was buried at Warri, where the Bishop had been importuned to leave a missionary. Thus the Church took possession for Christ!

APPENDIX

APPENDIX

WE reprint, by permission, from the *Life of Faith* and the *Record*, papers written by intimate friends in the first flush of bereavement, because they sparkle with personal touches ; and to them we append notes of an address by the Bishop himself. One lingers lovingly among the mass of skeleton sermons which he left behind ; but they are so truly *skeleton* that it would be impossible to reproduce them. The address given was taken down at the time, but contains little more than headings ; but it gives an idea of the real practical way in which he dealt with spiritual subjects. There was no "legal fiction" about salvation in his presentation of it. He proclaimed real deliverance from sin ; therefore souls in earnest welcomed his teaching.

REMINISCENCES OF A MISSIONARY FROM THE NIGER.

We first met at Lagos in 1892. His greeting was, "How are you, dear brother?" accompanied with that bright smile of his, and a cordial handshake.

The first thing I noticed was, that he was so fatherly and genial, especially to all the missionaries, ever thinking of the comfort and welfare of others. If any of us were not quite up to the mark, out would come the medicine chest, and we should be promptly doctored ; and, I must add, with remarkable success. Another thing was his utter contempt for conventionalities.

He was the life and brightness of our party ; his hearty laugh would peal out above all the rest. His loving, affectionate way won all our hearts, and we were delighted to serve him. Mrs. Hill, although quieter in manner, was equally loved by us all. She and her husband were essentially one in everything. They were pre-eminently "given to hospitality," and were never so glad as when surrounded by a happy circle of friends. But that which I appreciated more than all was the total absence of that rather stiff and proper English propriety. They were delightfully informal and *real* in all their intercourse with others.

I was also impressed by the real courtesy and gentleness with which he treated any African visitor. Nothing in his manner or demeanour would remind them that they were members of another race. If anything, with them he was slightly more punctilious than with Europeans, to avoid wounding their susceptibilities. It was simply wonderful how soon he seemed to win their love and confidence. Those who bitterly opposed his policy could not withstand the charm of his manner and presence. Yet beneath all this real kindness and courtesy of demeanour they knew that on a point of principle he would stand like a rock. He was ever ready to stand up for the oppressed ; and on one occasion, at least, came into very sharp collision with the "powers that be" on a question in which he thought the natives had not got fair play.

He was a first-rate cook, and very frequently cooked our dinner at Onitsha, bringing the dishes and putting them on the table amid a continual stream of happy, innocent fun. Nothing came amiss —marking out sites, planning buildings, climbing a tree to survey the country, writing, reading, preaching, doctoring ; he was, indeed, prepared unto every good work.

He lived in a little mud cottage, and seemed perfectly happy and contented while there, although he made it his first business to see that proper dwelling-houses were sent out for the new missionaries.

We all told him our secrets, and consulted him about our private affairs. He would listen with earnest sympathy, and spared himself no trouble to help us out of any difficulty—spiritual or temporal. On one occasion, when I was much exercised upon a question upon which I asked his advice, he got out of bed—we were both sleeping on deck—and paced the deck with me for at least a couple of hours.

He was a keen observer, and formed very rapid

judgments on the character of people with whom he came in contact. Where he trusted, he trusted implicitly.

Both the Bishop and Mrs. Hill's one thought seemed to be to minister to others—in any and every way. I remember going with him to visit a poor sick woman at Onitsha. How tenderly he tried to help her, and how trustfully she resigned herself to him, recognising in the look and touch that universal language of love.

Personal Recollections of the late Bishop Hill.

It is impossible to think of our friend as dead. Such a bright, vivid personality as his always suggests life—fulness of life; and we who mourn him at home, and did not see the fever overcome that strong physical frame, can only feel that mortality is swallowed up of life.

I remember when I first met him at Melbourne, and afterwards spent some time with him and dear Mrs. Hill in their happy home at Auckland, being struck with the rare combinations in his character. I keenly regretted leaving him in that narrow sphere where he was then working. No doubt his mental powers were being trained by contact with the quick-witted, practical colonists. His Sunday afternoon lectures to young men were crowded by eager listeners, and his choice of subjects was of the widest, embracing many social and intellectual questions of the day.

It was then, probably, that he acquired that habit of rapid and assimilative reading for which he was really remarkable. Like many omnivorous readers, he used to sit up very late at night, and would read steadily through at a sitting any new book that interested him. He was a delightful companion, a talker who could never weary or bore; there was such a freshness and originality in his way of looking at every question. There was nothing he liked better than to open out on some social or theological problem to a sympathetic listener. He was never afraid of paradox, and sometimes made the mistake of saying to an audience what should only have been said to one or two with whom he was intimate, thus causing himself to be misunderstood. His own nature was so generous that he expected generous treatment from others, even in criticism, and was bitterly disappointed when he found some word of his had hit the wrong mark through a want of understanding of the speaker's motives. But how is it possible to write adequately of one so all-round as he was—so practical and full of common sense, yet so intensely spiritually minded, so stern in his views of right, yet tender and sensitive as a woman—easily wounded, yet withal thoroughly manly and self-reliant?

His success in the administrative and organising work which fell to him in West Africa was due to that grasp of the question which has been well called in the *Times* notice *statesmanlike*; and that grasp was the result of a varied training, a conscientious impartiality in weighing and sifting facts and evidence, a habit, when once he saw a thing clearly, of going straight to the mark, and above all, a childlike reliance on the guidance of the Holy Ghost. I know of instances where this guidance was singularly marked and clear, but such confidences are sacred ground.

God used our beloved brother in many ways, but he was pre-eminently a winner of souls. To know him at his best and happiest it was necessary to go through a mission with him. No one had a more wonderful record of remarkable conversions. His experiences as a prison chaplain in New Zealand among murderers and convicts of all sorts have often strengthened my faith when depressed at the rejection of the Gospel. Lately his earnest pleading with sinners rather gave place to pleadings with the people of God for the souls in Africa; but the ultimate object was the same. His success in both cases surely lay in the fact that his love for souls was ever dominated and inspired by a higher love—his love for the Saviour of souls. With what glowing words he tried to stir the apathetic during those last weeks at home! How he thrilled us as he called upon men and women to come and die for Africa!

He preached as one with a message, and so his sermons were always original and forceful. I think it may be confidently asserted that no one ever slept through one. Yet his preaching was very unequal. It was impossible that it should be otherwise, for with such a sympathetic nature he was of course keenly susceptible to his surroundings. He never used a stereotyped phrase ; every word was struck off the anvil of his heart.

There was nothing narrow in our brother's theology ; he seemed to have a happy knack of embracing all that was beautiful and helpful from whatever source it came. His own grip of vital truth was too tenacious to make him fear to look at all sides, aye, and to stretch out helpful hands to those in mist and doubt.

No sketch of him would be accurate which did not give prominence to his strong hold upon the "blessed hope" as a life power. I happened one day to come into a friend's room, and found him in earnest converse with a godly doctor, an "exclusive." When Mr. Hill (it was before he was Bishop) had gone, the doctor said to me, with great satisfaction, "That young man has got the right thing in him," and much more to the same effect. No two men could have been more widely divergent on most points, yet they became great friends on the ground of their common faith in a coming Saviour.

One last word on Bishop Hill as a friend. He had every quality that goes to make the ideal friend—rarest constancy, true insight into character, unflinching faithfulness (I seem to hear his earnest voice saying so emphatically, "You're wrong!"), combined with the utmost tenderness and consideration, and a childlike humbleness when he recognised a superior mind; indeed, the beautiful, but now somewhat rare, quality of admiration was one of his most charming characteristics. Latterly, circumstances brought him into contact with some of the greatest minds in the Church, and he loved to talk in the unrestrained intercourse of friendship of his appreciation of this privilege. Generosity is a poor word to express the "abandon" of his affection. When he loved, it meant that he placed himself and all that he had at the disposal of his friend. Those who could call him by this hallowed name know that he cannot be replaced.

I cannot conclude this little sketch with words more beautiful and fitting than those of the Abbé Perreyve in his funeral oration over the younger Ampère:—"I do not fear to recall his beloved face, even in Thy presence, O Jesus! for Thou wert in Thy mortal days an incomparable Friend!"

R. E. F.

JOSEPH SIDNEY HILL, BISHOP.

I first met Bishop Hill in the autumn of 1890, after a service in a City church, in which I had addressed a gathering of young men. He was introduced to me, if I remember right, by Mr. Barlow of Islington. He interested me much with his account of mission work in Australia, and, finding that he was for the moment without any definite employment, and would like to know more of mission work in England, I invited him to a conference which was to be held the following week at Roxeth, Harrow. There I think that all the brethren present were struck by the spirituality and fervour of his remarks. I felt so much drawn to him myself that I sounded him about undertaking work in connection with the Church Parochial Mission Society, and to this he was subsequently appointed, at a salary that was little more than nominal. I had the great advantage of his assistance in four of my subsequent missions, when he took the work amongst the children and in other ways afforded valuable help. With the children he was particularly happy, and always succeeded in interesting them greatly; and I believe that many young hearts were won for the Lord while he thus worked for us. But happy as his connection with us was, he never concealed from me that he regarded it as only temporary in its character, and as a matter of fact it only lasted about a year.

It was in December 1891, during a revisit that I made in his company to St. Luke's, Wolverhampton, just a year after our happy united work there in the general Wolverhampton Mission, that he confided to me the fact that he had offered himself to the C.M.S. in the hope of being of some use in restoring harmony in that very disturbed mission on the Niger. I vividly recall the solemn way in which he spoke of the possible and even probable result of his offer. He had been so very near death before, owing to the effect of the climate on his constitution, that he seemed to have almost a presentiment that his mission would be his death. Yet, like a true Christian hero, he allowed no such consideration to move him; neither did he count his life dear, so long as he might be of some service to the cause that lay so near to his heart. So profound an impression did his words and his manner make upon me that when I heard subsequently of Bishop Crowther's death, one of the first thoughts that occurred to me was the hope that he might be appointed as his successor, chiefly because I thought that thus what I had learned to regard as a very valuable life might be spared. For he had given me to understand that he thought the chief danger for his health lay in the fact that his work would probably lie in the interior, where the pestilential marshes and the extreme roughness of the life would be likely to try him severely. I remember his saying that he did not think that he should run any very serious risk in the part of the country where Bishop Crowther at that time resided. So when I heard of his nomination for the bishopric I greatly rejoiced, regarding it as a reprieve for my dear friend. Alas! how little did I think that this expectation was to be falsified within the first few weeks of his assumption of his episcopal functions! But I shall never forget the calm and unostentatious way in which he deliberately faced the probability of an early death, laying, without a murmur or a regret, his all upon the altar. I should, perhaps, mention, as a somewhat remarkable coincidence, that just at this time, when there was no thought of a vacancy in that remote diocese, about a week after he had offered himself to the C.M.S. for the Niger, he was sounded about a bishopric in a much more salubrious and attractive part of the world, where he might have escaped from all apprehensions as to probable injury to his health; but he had offered himself to God for work that promised plenty of difficulty and hardship, and probably much worry and annoyance, and, having put his hand to the plough, he would not look back.

Recollections crowd in upon my mind as I thus write of my dear departed friend. I think of his bright face and his genial smile, of his quick and ready sympathy and his capacity of encouragement. Humble and modest to the last degree, there was yet a latent power in the man, which had already begun to work itself to the surface in his all too brief episcopate. To know him was to love him, but to know him better was both to love and admire him; and the admiration would, I am persuaded, have been very generally felt had it pleased the inscrutable providence of God to spare him to his diocese for even a few years. But God knows best! That dear face is no longer to carry its witness of inward peace and joy to careworn, sorrowing sinners; and that voice, so full of earnest feeling, no longer to plead with human ears and hearts. But the sacrifice has not been made in vain. There is seed sown in that freshly-closed tomb with its double burden, where he and his dear wife, lovely and pleasant in their lives, in their death are not divided, that will carry its harvest in that far land some future day, when possibly the story of his brief episcopate is almost forgotten. I cannot help recalling to-day the text from which I spoke to young men in the city on the evening of the very day on which I had made his acquaintance: "To what purpose is this waste?" Christ alone knows the full answer to that question; but as the house was filled with the odour of that ointment then, so is the Christian world to-day redolent with the fragrance of such sacrificed lives. Pericles was right when he said, "Of noble men every nation is the monumental tomb," and the Church of Christ may equally say that each successful mission, each race or tribe or community brought from heathen darkness into the light of the Gospel day, is an eternal monument to the men who, either by their martyr-like lives or by their martyr-like deaths, have contributed to the bringing about of this blessed result.

W. HAY M. H. AITKEN.

CLEANSING.

BY THE LATE BISHOP HILL.

"And the Lord said unto Joshua, Get thee up, wherefore liest thou thus upon thy face?" (JOSHUA vii. 10, 11).

BELOVED brethren, I want first of all to impress upon my own self and yourselves this fact—that there are infinite possibilities of a holy life in the power of the

Cross of the Lord Jesus Christ and of God the Holy Ghost. If we are not holy, it is not God's fault; if we are not free from sin and sin's power, it is not God's fault.

Now there is something Joshua must do if Israel would be cleansed from their sin, and if they would have the victory. They must put away from themselves the accursed thing. Now I know nothing about your lives, but I want you to see this—if your life is a life of failure, of bondage to sin, of continual confession of committed sins, that it is no use your asking God's forgiveness for your sins to-day, and then to-morrow to do the same thing. By doing so you are making use of the Lord Jesus Christ's sacrifice in such a way as to make it a stumbling-block in your own lives.

It was never intended that that one and all-sufficient sacrifice for sin should warrant a sort of personal indulgence in personal sin. Now we want to deal with ourselves thoroughly, and I ask you whether it is not true that you have found it easy to sin because you knew there was an easy way to get forgiveness? (See Psalm li. 2.)

Do you want to be thoroughly cleansed in God's sight? I remember a remark made not long ago by a devoted brother. Some one asked a question as to the possibilities of holiness, and he answered in one brief sentence (which I want to impress upon you) something like this, "You can be just as holy as you like to be."

I want you to see that holiness is utterly impossible apart from God, and that it is utterly impossible in us apart from ourselves.

Cleansing from Sin.

There are different ways of being cleansed from sin, and I want to bring this subject before you. Some say it is all in one text, and yet they use that text in the wrong way. You know the passage in 1 John i. 17: "If we walk in the light as He is in the light, we have fellowship one with another; and the blood of Jesus Christ His Son cleanseth us from all sin." Now I want you to deal with this passage in connection with the one I have just read, where you find God saying to Joshua, "Get up." It is not on your knees that this question is to be dealt with. "Get up," and put that accursed thing away; and then Israel can be cleansed.

Cleansing by Blood.

I am afraid we often speak of the blood in this way: we look upon our sins as though they were recorded upon a slate, and we think that the action of the blood can wash and blot them out.

There is another thing you must do before that takes place. It is perfectly true that God will do that, but He only blots away sin when He sees that condition of the soul which permits Him to do so.

Do you know that you cannot forgive your child just when you like? You have no business to unconditionally forgive your child when you know that he has done wrong. There is some moral condition on which that child must approach you, and then, and only then, can you forgive him. I want to impress upon you this fact—that the Lord Jesus Christ Himself is the one and all-sufficient Sacrifice. How did the Jew become a partaker of the blessings of a sacrifice? By *identification.* When the Jew put his sin upon the lamb, when the priest put his sin on the lamb, when he confessed his sin before the people upon the lamb, that lamb was identified with himself. Now, "He who knew no sin was made sin for us." We become righteous by identification with His righteousness. But what does it mean? That is the point.

I want to be quite plain. There was no such thing in Israel as forgiveness by blood, or cleansing by blood, without the use of the knife. Without shedding of blood there was no remission, and there is no such thing as forgiveness of sin in your soul, without that action of the knife, without your dying to sin. If you imagine that, by going on your knees and asking God to forgive you your sin, whilst at the same time you are determined to continue in it, I tell you, in God's name, you get up from your knees more condemned than if you had never heard the gospel. I believe one of the curses of the day is the claptrap preaching of forgiveness that does not change the moral life.

So subtle is the power of Satan that I believe there are hundreds of Christians who indulge in sin because they think they can get a cheap forgiveness. God will not thus be mocked.

When God sees a man as before Him dealing with sin and turning his back upon it, and looking to Him for mercy through Jesus Christ, there is forgiveness. There is no such thing as forgiveness apart from crucifixion of sin. Salvation is through a crucified Saviour, and the condition of your salvation is that you be crucified with Christ; or, in other words, the cleansing by blood is yours on condition of your death to sin. God cannot die to sin for you; you must die for yourself. He can meet your guilt by means of the Substitute, but the death is an experience that you yourself must voluntarily accept, and in doing so you cut yourself from sin.

Cleansing by Restitution.

Turn to Leviticus vi. 1-5. I had a little boy in my class who stole my pencil. Suppose that boy knelt and asked forgiveness for having stolen that pencil, and yet kept the pencil in his pocket, do you think God would forgive him? What must he do? He must restore the thing that he has stolen. If you have told a person an untruth, what must you do? You must go and tell that person the truth, if you want forgiveness. In your business life you have taken advantage of another, and deceived your neighbour, and you want forgiveness: how are you going to get it? Kneel down and ask for it? Yes, but go first and make restitution, my brother. Until we get some righteous idea of God's dealing with our souls we are not likely to be very righteous in our conduct towards others.

There are men who wonder why they have not power with God. There is a thick cloud between God and them. Until that question of sin has been dealt with, believe me, though your soul may be saved, and you may get to heaven, you will get there alone. Oh! our God is a holy God, and a righteous God. I have come across people who have talked so flippantly about these things, and I have known these very people in their business to be guilty of transactions that most of the world would be ashamed of. If you have told a lie to anyone, tell them you told a lie. Go yourself and tell them: God will not go—you must. I was preaching at a church one day when the curate brought me a letter which he had received from his father. He had written to his father and confessed a lie which he had told him when a boy, and had got forgiveness. "Now," he said, "I know what real peace is."

Cleansing by the Water of Separation.

See Numbers xix. 9—"And it shall be kept . . . for a water of separation: it is a purification for sin;" and associate with it John xiii. 10 to 14. How many of you understand the washing of one another's feet?

What is it?

"Wash ye one another's feet." If you study Numbers xix. you will find that there was a kind of defilement that takes place by coming in contact with sin. Suppose you are employed in a shop, warehouse, or manufactory where there are a great number of ungodly people you are forced to come in contact with every day. You may go into the warehouse or workshop in the morning, and say to yourselves, "Thank God for His blessed truths. I am washed, cleansed, and sanctified." But before you have been there many minutes perhaps an oath is uttered, perhaps vulgar words are used, perhaps you are chaffed. Does that have any effect upon you? It has—an effect that may be put all right by the Lord Jesus Christ Himself. We in the mission field who come in contact with the heathen, with the darkness and demon worship, know that there is an effect produced upon the soul. Sometimes it brings us in humbleness before God. If you are defiled there is a way of getting rid of that defilement. Just as we get defiled with evil, so we get restored and brought back again when, by the blessedness of fellowship, we are brought in close contact with true believers.

Cleansing by the Washing of Water by the Word.

If you will turn to Ephesians v. 26, you will find another cleansing: "That He might sanctify and cleanse it with the washing of water by the

Word." What does that mean? If you look at 2 Corinthians you will find that when Moses was with God the mind of God was reflected in his countenance. His heart felt it and his face showed it.

The glory of God must manifest itself. The Word of God transforms the mind. The mind is led captive to the mind of Christ until your own thoughts are changed into God's thoughts, and your mind into God's mind. The mind is brought into captivity by the washing (of the water of the Word of God).

Cleansing by Fire.

See Isaiah vi. 6—"Then flew one of the Seraphims unto me, having a live coal in his hand, which he had taken with the tongs from off the altar; and he laid it on my mouth, and said, Lo, this hath touched thy lips; and thine iniquity is taken away, and thy sin is purged." Also Luke iii. 16—"I indeed baptize you with water, but . . . He shall baptize you with the Holy Ghost and with fire."

Fire purges away the dross. The action of fire upon the soul is this: it raises the standard of holiness by putting into the mind God's standard of holiness. It is only when God's ways are put in place of our ways that we are purged with fire, and the pure mind comes out in our lives.

14

CLEANSING BY PURGING.

Look at John xv. 2—"Every branch in Me that beareth not fruit He taketh away; and every branch that beareth fruit He purgeth it, that it may bring forth more fruit."

I knew a gentleman in London who used to be a Methodist class-leader. After a time he became a wealthy man, and joined a fashionable church. His wealth after a time seemed to cut out the very spiritual part of his soul. Now we find him walking the streets of London a pauper.

What a purging that soul needed! The sap is the source of the fruit, and the pruning takes place that the sap may be more effectual in producing fruit.

CLEANSING BY SATAN.

1 Tim. i. 20, and 1 Corinthians v. 5—"Delivered unto Satan." "To deliver such an one unto Satan for the destruction of the flesh, that the spirit may be saved in the day of the Lord Jesus." Oh, my brothers! this is an awful thought. If God cannot cleanse you by the water of separation, by fire, and by purging, there will be the pangs of the chastisement of the devil. You must be cleansed. He must present you. You must be spotless. If one thing will not do it another must. If we are not cleansed we must turn and be amended. There is a sort of thing that passes muster as an ideal of cleansing: but is your soul cleansed as God intended? Is it up to the

standard of God's truth? Is it pure? You had better die than sin. You had better die than be dishonest in that business of yours. I pray you bring your life to the test of God's truth. Is it clean in God's sight? If not, whose fault is it? It is not God's fault. There is the Cross; there is the life; there is the gift of the Holy Spirit of God. The Spirit's work is to sanctify you, to make you like Christ; and the only question is, will you take Christ? Keep your eye on Him, and you will never find yourself in hopeless despair.

I ask you, are you cleansed? Deal with just that thing. If it is a bad temper you have got, if it is a habit of exaggeration, if you are just a little careless with regard to what you consider trifles, if you have a little secret indulgence, if you are vain, or if you are proud, just bring it all to the light, just bring it to Jesus. Then you will find a joy and a gladness that will fill your soul. It will be like unto a well of water springing up in the fulness of life.

Here are a few pungent sentences from Bishop Hill's address to the student volunteers on soul winning.

" *Love.*—The first essential of all spiritual work, the greatest of all gifts, is love—not our love to God, but the love of God in us (1 Cor. xiii.). There is such a condition of soul in which we can be a possessor of God's love for souls, and we can love the heathen with something of the same love as our Lord Himself. I don't believe that any one is used to the salvation of souls who has not this gift of love. There are many here who are fully developed in the intellectual side of their nature; but there is this other thing which is so necessary. There is nothing that touches another man so much as sympathy.

"*Broken-heartedness.*—The man that is going to be a soul winner must be a broken-hearted man. We may reap what other men have sown, but we won't both sow and reap ourselves unless we have a broken heart. There was a time when I was not used for the salvation of souls, because I got under the influence of the theories of the day in reference to the condition of the lost hereafter. I began to think there was some way by which God would bring men out of eternal darkness, and that sapped all the earnestness out of me; and until I began to know about weeping over the lost as Jesus wept over a lost city I was no use. We want to keep before us this—that men are perishing, and that they are lost to God. It is a loss to God, not only to the soul.

"*Waiting on God* (Luke xxiv. 49).—The only way in which you can be positive that the message you are going to give will result in the salvation of souls is, when you have tarried and waited until God Himself has given you the message. Tarry ye until God has fitted, qualified, equipped you for what you have to do. Don't go to a meeting and talk to souls until first you have talked to God, and God has talked to you. The man most used is just the man who has realised God's grace in pardoning him.

"*Prompt Obedience* (Acts viii. 26).—Prompt obedience to the Spirit of God is a most essential thing in soul winning.

"*Faith.*—'I am not ashamed of the Gospel of Christ.' Believe in the efficacy of the blood to save, and believe in the power of the Word of God just to do what God has promised it shall do. In dealing privately with souls, if you have not the most perfect confidence in the Word, it is detected by the soul with whom you are dealing.

"*Decision.*—Here comes the sphere of prayer. Decision is something you had better not interfere with too much. Let God do it, not you. There *is* a little value in brains in evangelistic work. To be clear and not to muddle up the soul is of tremendous value. In other words, don't be in a hurry, take a little time. Don't rush the poor soul through, and don't get him excited. I have had to say to an excitable man, Sit quite still, and don't say a word. Always get a man to do something. Don't leave him where he was. Bring him a little way, and if need be let him come again."

The following testimony from Mr. Eugene Stock we gladly insert, regretting that it arrived too late to be incorporated earlier in the book :—

BISHOP HILL AND THE C.M.S.

It may be frankly acknowledged that the suggestion, first made by Mr. Aitken, that J. S. Hill should be nominated to the Archbishop of Canterbury for the bishopric vacant by the death of Samuel Crowther, came as a surprise to us. But this was because we did not know the man then. Some of us remembered him as a very fervent, but (from the point of view of a grave Committee) somewhat volatile, student at the Church Missionary College sixteen years before, and also as a missionary to Africa who had quickly broken down in the insidious climate of the West Coast; but that he should be a bishop, and, especially, a bishop in West Africa, was an unlooked-for proposal indeed. But when the suggestion was made, he had already offered himself for the Niger Mission, and had been accepted by the Society. This should never be forgotten. Hill's return to the land where he had long ago broken down was not because a bishopric was offered him. His desire was to go back to the field of his earliest efforts in the capacity of a simple missionary. It was a trying time on the Niger: Bishop Crowther was in feeble health; Robinson was dead; Graham Brooke was alone at Lokoja; and many leading African Christians were dissatisfied with the Society's recent course of action. Hill longed to be the bearer of an olive-branch. He united the highest standard of spirituality with a singularly forbearing spirit; like his Divine Master, he hated sin and loved the sinner; and he thought he might be used of God to heal wounds which were none the less painful because they had been thought to be necessary. Then came the news of Bishop Crowther's death, and then of Graham Brooke's. The C.M.S. Committee took the best step possible to ascertain Hill's fitness for the bishopric by writing out to New Zealand to inquire of their old and honoured friend, himself once a missionary in India, Bishop Stuart of Waiapu. The testimony received in reply was decisive; and closer personal intercourse with Hill himself resulted in a general feeling, "Can we find such an one as this is, a man in whom the Spirit of God is?" His name was submitted to the Archbishop of Canterbury; and the Archbishop at once perceived in him the wisdom and the devotion so indispensable for such a bishopric. It was the Primate's own suggestion that he should go out first on a temporary visit as Bishop Designate and Archbishop's Commissary; and the remarkable sagacity and tact which he manifested while executing this special commission proved to all that God had graciously led the Society to the right man for the vacant see.

I myself was absent in Australasia all this time. In New Zealand I constantly heard of Hill's name and influence, and met some who avowed that they owed their conversion, under God, to him. I returned to England just at the same time that he returned from his temporary visit to West Africa in April 1893. On the 25th of that month he met the "Group Committee" which specially supervises the C.M.S. African Missions. From 11 a.m. to 5 p.m. they sat, in close and careful and prayerful consideration of the many difficult problems connected with the position at the time in West Africa. Never shall I forget the patience and thoughtfulness and wisdom with which Hill discussed the various questions. It was a new revelation to me. I had known him only as a fervent evangelist. I now saw him as a statesman. As the hours went by, I could only mentally exclaim, "Thank God for such a man!"

Many other reminiscences might be given, both of his work in Committees and of the more congenial work of pleading for Africa in meeting after meeting in all parts of England. At the Keswick Convention of that year, which he attended with his two African Assistant-Bishops, three weeks after the consecration, his humility, and the total absence in him of *self*, were a lesson to us all. He took no prominent part; but he went in and out among the "student volunteers," and was the cheeriest and brightest in their camp. He would not speak at the great Saturday missionary meeting, but asked that Bishop Oluwole might be put up instead. But he offered the concluding prayer at that wonderful gathering, and seemed to take us all, as it were, by the hand, and lead us close up to the throne of God.

The Gleaners' Union Anniversary on November 1st, at which Bishop Hill presided, is referred to in the foregoing pages. It was memorable for Mrs. Bishop's great speech, which, in print, has ever since been circulating literally by hundreds of thousands. Her concluding words were, "May He touch all our hearts with the spirit of self-sacrifice, and with the inspiration of that love of His, which, when He came to redeem the world, *kept nothing back*." It was in sympathy with those words that the Bishop gave, at the end, his last message to a great London audience—that solemn message which is printed on a preceding page. But between Mrs. Bishop's speech and his there came two others, one by a kindred spirit, the Rev. H. B. Macartney, of Melbourne, and the other by a young aspirant for missionary service, the Rev. W. A. C. Fremantle. Although Fremantle was only allowed twelve minutes, I pulled him down before they were over, in order to give Bishop Hill time for his last words. We little thought that by the time the next Gleaners' Anniversary came round, both the young Oxford man and the new Bishop would receive their call to the presence of the Lord. Dear Fremantle, too, "kept nothing back." He gave up much, a wide circle of influential friends and the highest prospects of usefulness, to go forth at the Lord's command;

and the Lord called him home exactly a year after that memorable meeting.

Then came the touching farewell at Euston, father and mother tenderly embracing the two young daughters left behind; and as the Liverpool train moved away, our hopes rose high for the Missions in West Africa. Six weeks passed away; Christmas came and went; the new year 1894 opened; and then, on the Epiphany, Saturday, January 6th, came the crushing telegram, "*Bishop Hill and Mrs. Hill at rest.*" Rarely have the C.M.S. Committee been so moved as when the solemn tidings were officially communicated to them at their meeting on the following Tuesday. After united prayer led by the Rev. C. G. Baskerville (who himself has given a son to Africa), the following minute was adopted unanimously:—

"In deepest sorrow, and with fullest trust in Him that doeth all things well, the Committee receive the intelligence of the home call of the Right Rev. Joseph Sidney Hill, D.D., Bishop in Western Equatorial Africa, and of Mrs. Hill, which occurred just as the Bishop was entering on the peculiarly difficult and responsible duties of the office for the fulfilment of which he appeared to be singularly gifted and prepared of God.

"He went out with a clearly defined and statesman-like policy, and with loving desire for the development of the Church under African leaders.

"Mr. Hill received at the Church Missionary College his training for the mission field, and was ordained and appointed to Lagos, whither he went out with Mrs. Hill in the year 1876, but was speedily invalided home.

"In 1878 he was transferred to the New Zealand Mission, and in 1882 resigned his connection with the Society, important evangelistic work amongst English-speaking people having opened up before him there.

"In New Zealand he developed, in marked degree, powers of organisation and influence. With much gentleness he combined unusual strength of character and strict conscientiousness, while his great power of sympathy, and his judicious tact, won the affection and confidence of those who had the privilege of knowing him.

"After his return to England, Mr. Hill was accepted by the Society for work on the Niger in November 1891, and was appointed Director of the whole of the Niger Mission. In the following May, before he had entered on his onerous charge, he was nominated to the Niger bishopric. At the desire of the Archbishop of Canterbury, who accepted the nomination, Mr. Hill went out in the first instance before consecration; his Grace appointed him his Commissary, and desired that on his return from a visit of inspection and inquiry he should report on the condition of things in the Niger Churches, with a special view to determine the character of the Episcopal supervision to be adopted there. During this visit his resourcefulness acquired in Colonial life was markedly manifest.

"The outcome of this visit, and of the report brought home by Mr. Hill, was his consecration, on St. Peter's Day, June 29th, 1893, at St. Paul's Cathedral, as Bishop in Western Equatorial Africa. At the same time the two African clergymen, the Rev. Isaac Oluwole and the Rev. Chas. Phillips, were, on his recommendation, consecrated as his assistants.

"In Mrs. Hill, whose missionary zeal equalled that of her husband, the female workers on the Niger were looking forward to welcome a truly valuable, efficient, and sympathetic counsellor and guide.

"That persons apparently possessing so unique equipment for a unique work should have been suddenly called away, is one of those mysteries the full solution of which the Great Day alone will make clear.

"The Committee would humbly pray for themselves, and for the missionaries, and for the African Christians in the wide area bereft of the Episcopal supervision of their dear friend, that this sore bereavement may result in such an increase of mutual sympathy, such an establishment of mutual confidence, and such a growing sense of dependence on the Great Head of the Church, as they doubt not it is designed under the teaching of God the Holy Spirit to produce.

"They humbly depend on God the Holy Spirit for needed grace and guidance in view of the many questions which will now have to be met regarding the future supervision of the work.

"They put on record their affectionate and sincere sympathy for the two young daughters thus sadly bereft of their parents, and would commit them with confiding trust to the sure mercies of the Father of the fatherless.

"The Committee desire that a copy of this minute be sent to the members of the family, and that they be assured of the Committee's sincere and prayerful sympathy with them, and especially with Miss Leachman, the devoted sister of Mrs. Hill, to whom the charge of the children was committed."

The following letter from the Archbishop of Canterbury was read at the meeting :—

"ADDINGTON PARK, CROYDON, *January 8th*, 1894.

"MY DEAR MR. WIGRAM,—

"I feel indeed utterly stricken by this terrible news from Lagos. So much arrangement and deliberation and work on the part of so many earnest minds seems utterly lost—but κατ' ἄνθρωπον λέγω. That is the comfort and strength. We shall see God bring some new force out of our defeat, and accomplish all in His own way. We merely are dumb at the mysteriousness of the bar in what seemed His working. . . . Those poor children!

"Ever yours sincerely,

"E. CANTUAR."

But the Lord's mysterious dealings were not yet finished. Telegram after telegram arrived announcing further deaths. Edgar Mathias (a Cambridge man ordained by Bishop Hill himself), James Vernall, Florence Mansbridge, A. E. Sealey, one after another were called away; Miss Maxwell was invalided home (though she has since bravely gone out again); and Bishop Hill's Niger party was reduced to one man, the Rev. C. E. Watney. "What I do thou knowest not now, but thou shalt know hereafter." But one thing we do know even now—know without a doubt: and that is, GOD IS LOVE!

E. S.

Letters poured in from every quarter bearing grateful testimony to Bishop Hill's character and work. One strain runs through them all, best expressed by Bishop Oluwole in one pregnant sentence: "My acquaintanceship with him was *a school of love, kindness, devotion, and thorough unselfishness.* May I not have learnt the lesson in vain!"

This is Africa's testimony to the man who bore her in his heart. May this brief record of his life be to many as a handbook in that "*school of love.*"

The last word shall be spoken by a Gleaner about the "Gleaners' own Missionary." The poem closes with a question; shall the immediate and practical result of reading this brief story of a true and full life be to furnish an answer?

IN MEMORIAM: J. S. H. AND L. H.

"When the morning was now come, Jesus stood on the shore.
—ST. JOHN xxi. 4.

He has toiled for his Master nobly
  On the far-off foreign strand;
Patiently joining the broken nets
  With a skilled and loving hand.
Now let him fling them far and wide
O'er Afric's dark and surging tide.

So they sped him forth rejoicing,
  The friends who loved him best—
The right man to the right place sent!
  Trust God with all the rest.
And his wife will take the true wife's part—
Strengthen his hands and cheer his heart.

They gave him the "fisher's coat,"
  Garb of a calling high,
With holy consecrating prayers,
  In the Minster solemnly.
Did no ear catch a whispered word?—
"He girds it on to meet his Lord!"

Farewell to the shores of England!
  They fade with the day's last beam;
And Afric's coast lies faintly blue
  In the misty morning gleam.
See! *Who* stands there in the twilight dim?
It is One who waits, and waits for him.

They knew not that it was Jesus
  Watching and waiting there;
But Faith has eagle eyes to see,
  And love is quick to hear.
Those listening hearts have caught the word—
Their eyes have seen—"It is the Lord."

They have braved the dark, cold death-wave,
  They are nearing the shining strand,
The Master, Whom they haste to meet,
  Holds fast each trembling hand.
Passed, from life's tossing, troubled sea,
To the fair, firm shore of Eternity.

But the nets—Oh! who shall grasp them
  And fling them out again?
Oh! who will toil in those waters dim,
  Fishing for souls of men;
To draw them in, a freight unpricèd,
And lay them at the Feet of Christ?

February 16th, 1894. M. M.

Printed by Hazell, Watson, & Viney, Ld., London and Aylesbury.